ADVANCE PRAISE FOR

WRITING BEYOND RECOGNITION

Queer Re-Storying for Social Change

"During a week when I had more than enough to do, I kept returning to Claire Robson's lively and engaging book *Writing Beyond Recognition*. Her theory of writing practice and wise pedagogy for transforming traumatic memory into story shows the importance of the creative arts for survival and resilience."

Ann Cvetkovich, Carleton University
author of *An Archive of Feelings and Depression: A Public Feeling*

WRITING BEYOND RECOGNITION

Queer Singularities: LGBTQ Histories, Cultures, and Identities in Education

Dennis J. Sumara, PhD, *Editor*

Queer Singularities takes an intersectional approach to exploring how normative and non-normative experiences of gender, race, class, and sexuality are taught and learned within lesbian, gay, bisexual, transgendered, and queer histories, cultures and identities.

Focused on processes and experiences of formal and informal education, books in the series will cover critical perspectives on topics such as schooling and sexuality, heteronormativity and learning, activism and curriculum, homophobia and trauma, urbanization and identity, and culture and creativity.

Through these exploratory juxtapositions, Queer Singularities aims to explore the paradoxical ways LGBTQ histories, cultures and identities are both productively singular and disruptively queer. In so doing, books in the series will provide new theoretical lenses and practical information for researchers, educators, leaders, and policy maker.

Published and Forthcoming Titles

Writing Beyond Recognition: Queer Re-Storying for Social Change
by Claire Robson (2021)
Our Children are Your Students: LGBTQ Families Speak Out
by Tara Goldstein (2020)
On Liking the Other: Queer Subjects and Religious Discourses
by Kevin J. Burke (2021)

The series editor, Dennis J. Sumara, PhD, invites individuals to submit proposals for any book-length manuscript, including but not restricted to the following:

- monographs
- textbooks
- edited collections
- primers
- readers
- anthologies
- handbooks
- conference proceedings

Prospectus guidelines can be found here: http://myersedpress.com/sites/stylus/MEP/Docs/Prospectus%20Guidelines%20MEP.pdf. If you have a project that you wish to have considered for publication, please send a proposal, one or two sample chapters, and your current CV to: Chris Myers, Publisher, Myers Education Press (c.myers@myersedpress.com).

WRITING BEYOND RECOGNITION

Queer Re-Storying
for Social Change

BY
CLAIRE ROBSON

Myers
Education
Press

GORHAM, MAINE

Myers
Education
Press

Copyright © 2021 | Myers Education Press, LLC

Published by Myers Education Press, LLC
P.O. Box 424 Gorham, ME 04038

Myers Education Press is an academic publisher specializing in books, e-books, and digital content in the field of education. All of our books are subjected to a rigorous peer review process and produced in compliance with the standards of the Council on Library and Information Resources.

Library of Congress Cataloging-in-Publication Data available from Library of Congress.

13-digit ISBN 978-1-9755-0419-9 (paperback)
13-digit ISBN 978-1-9755-0418-2 (hardcover)
13-digit ISBN 978-1-9755-0420-5 (library networkable e-edition)
13-digit ISBN 978-1-9755-0421-2 (consumer e-edition)

Printed in the United States of America.

All first editions printed on acid-free paper that meets the American National Standards Institute Z39-48 standard.

Books published by Myers Education Press may be purchased at special quantity discount rates for groups, workshops, training organizations, and classroom usage. Please call our customer service department at 1-800-232-0223 for details.

Cover design by Teresa Lagrange.
Image courtesy of pexels.com

Visit us on the web at www.myersedpress.com to browse our complete list of titles.

CONTENTS

Contents

LIST OF TABLES AND FIGURES

INTRODUCTION

DENNIS SUMARA
Queer Singularities Series Editor

WRITING BEYOND RECOGNITION IS a book about how teachers can create conditions for learners to reconcile their fear of being ordinary with their desire to belong. Informed by critical arts-based research methods and Robson's extensive experience as a writer of memoir, *Writing Beyond Recognition* takes the reader on a journey of what it means for people to give testimony and bear witness to their lives.

The idea and practice of ironic paradox guides the purpose and mission of the *Queer Singularities* book series. This first volume in the series by Claire Robson is a vivid and important introduction to the complexities of what it means to be ironically, paradoxically, and singularly queer. Robson's volume, like others that will follow in this series, is focused on demonstrating the complex ways that experiences and expressions of identity can exist both inside and outside normative conceptions of gender, sexuality, class, and race.

The title *Writing Beyond Recognition* points to Robson's primary argument that one must learn how to use existing language forms within new practices in order to see one's implication the existing social and cultural order. Through her use of critical arts research and teaching practices she shows why we must become somewhat suspicious about what is concealed in epic coming out stories that can become in themselves somewhat normative. This, and other topics and arguments in the book, deepens our understanding of how heteronormativity and homophobia constrain not only what we can *be* but also what we can *know*.

I have known Claire Robson for 20 years and have come to appreciate and admire her keen intellect, pedagogical prowess and community-based research impacts. During the time I worked with her in my capacity as Editor on this book, I came to deeply value and appreciate her ability to author

a text that in itself enables transformative change. I caution the reader that
Robson's vivid writing will take you inside her and her participant's and
student's stories in ways that are both unsettling and illuminating. That
journey of reading and thinking has shifted my perceptions in powerful and
important ways—exactly what a great book should do.

OPENING

In many ways, writing is an unnatural and antisocial activity, and by extension, so are writers. Like spiders, we crouch in some quiet corner and spin out lines of *stuff*, which is generated somewhere inside us as if by some mysterious, unnamed organ. If we are lucky, these lines that we extrude join together to make shapes and structures, like webs. These tenuous compositions feel like home to us, but for everyone else, they are traps. Right now, for instance, I am hoping that you are tempted. I have spun some lines and baited them with a little story. I am waiting for you to set just one foot down...

The spider's web is pretty, but pound for pound, it is stronger than steel or Kevlar and much more elastic. Even those who study it cannot reproduce it. The spider's artful filaments seem decorative and flimsy, but they feed and support the world's most resilient population, who live in almost every terrestrial habitat on earth. Like stories, spiders' webs are adaptive, patched, worked over, reinvented. And like stories, they are everywhere.

This book is about acts of learning about ourselves and others through rethinking the stories we have spun about ourselves and the stories others have told about us. It is about how telling our stories can change our minds about what happened and challenge the ways we are seen by others and the ways that history has been constructed. It is about processes of constant destruction and rebuilding. Though writing is a mysterious act, there are many things to be known and understood about it. Though it is often a solitary act, it has the ability to create and change communities. I write this book in large part to demystify the act of writing and to challenge the myth of individual God-given talent.

I believe that everyone has a story to tell. Every story is unique. The best person to tell that story is the one who lived it, and anyone can do this work, whatever their age or educational background. The things we really need to know about writing are not to do with form, rhyme schemes, vocabulary, and narrative structure. These are necessary parts of craft, and thinking about them is helpful. But writing does not start there. It starts inside, with that mysterious organ that processes our memories and turns them into images and inspirations that stretch out feelers to touch a signal strand in the web of our consciousness. It is then that we must be alert and ready to pounce. It is then that we draw upon less tangible authorial qualities, the ones you will never find in a how-to book. They include honesty, humility, patience, and courage.

I cannot claim to teach these qualities in a book, but I have thought a lot over the years about the pedagogical structures that support this kind of work and the strong communities of change that are supported by it in turn. Most of what I know I learned on the job, with the help of those I have worked with - writers, artists, poets, activists, filmmakers, dancers, and my students, young and old. Their work informs this book, particularly in the strong practice examples that illustrate each of its four sections.

The first section is about memory, how it works, and how it can be opened up, unpacked, and investigated. The second section is about recognition – what happens when one opens up one's memories, and what might prevent you from doing so. The third section is about revising, which I frame as a process of homing in on the intention of the work. In the fourth and final section, I consider the business of representation – the ways we choose to show the products of our work to others. Running through all these sections is the notion of collectivity. Here, I am indebted to Kelly Oliver's work on witnessing, acknowledged in my book title, *Beyond Recognition*. I am grateful to her for new and more optimistic ways of thinking about subjectivity and the impact of trauma. Though Oliver does not minimize the capacity of trauma to damage the fabric of human life, she does believe that it can be repaired through acts of witnessing. These acts require that life experiences be revisited, recollected, and represented, but crucially, they must also be understood and felt. Witnessing moves beyond recognition as it invites empathy, understanding, and change, both individual and social. Critical arts practices, I will argue, serve that large agenda. They are powerful acts of hope – that histories can be revised and futures improved through making art together.

I thank everyone who has walked this journey with me – the kids in rural libraries, the people who came to my retreats, the students in my classes in high schools and universities, the elders and youth who collaborated with me on so many exciting and disruptive projects. You have been my teachers, and you always made the lessons interesting and fun. Finally, I thank my friend, colleague, and editor, Dennis Sumara for his wise counsel, his sharp and mercurial mind, and his faith in my work.

PART I

REMEMBERING

CHAPTER ONE

Memory

O UR SENSE OF WHO we are is an aspect of our consciousness—a shifting and present awareness of our existence largely composed of our recollections of the past and our projections into the future. As meaning-making animals, we stitch these memories and desires together to form a sense of continuous self. We know that we are discrete individuals because we can recall our specific and unique histories or, at least, their most significant aspects. Although these memories are not entirely reliable, because they are subject to interpretation and forgetfulness, most of us feel that our recollections of our lived experiences are robust enough to generate a sense of solid identity. Our sense of who we are also depends on the stories others tell about us. Our parents fill in details of our childhood we may have forgotten; our friends, teachers, partners, and children reflect our strengths and draw attention to our failures. In this way, our sense of ourselves is relational.

The young female narrator in the story that follows learns about her status and standing in the family through both the spoken and unspoken behaviors of her parents and her brother. I shall use her story, my story, as a first case study and an illustration of this book's purpose—to think about making art from our memories and how this contributes to social and personal change.

"Privet"

Everything is back to front at our house. All function is hidden. Behind the bungalow, like muddy shoes discarded at the door, are the vegetable plots and the fruit canes, the rainwater barrel and the compost heap, the swing and the air raid shelter. The front garden is for show. Flowers bloom obediently around a smooth lawn. A pixie fishes in eternal disappointment from his grey stone mushroom. It is a cold and clipped landscape.

Like the dog and the horse, the privet bush enjoys a unique relationship with Man, who has bent its evolution to his purposes. It seems like privet was born to be pruned into a state of absolute regularity. Over the years, my father has trained its slender branches and tiny green leaves into such perfect squareness that it is more like a piece of furniture than anything organic. It provides a final, impenetrable barrier to the eyes of the street.

My mother is in a bad mood. I can tell by the way she cracks the eggs into the frying pan and they spit and curl into white lace. My father sits silently at the end of the table in his best thorn-proof wool suit. He sucks the end of his pencil and studies his crossword. I have worked out for myself what a cross word is. My mother's chair is nearest the cooker, and Michael and I face each other across the table. Our aunts and uncles say Michael has our father's noble features—his straight nose and navy-blue eyes. He has a brand-new briefcase like Dad's too, and a white shirt and a red tie and a Dr. Who pencil case.

"Go and get the tomato ketchup, Claire," my mother says. "You're old enough to set the table properly. Your dad likes ketchup."

"I like ketchup too," says Michael. "I need lots of food for my brains, because I'm going to school."

When Michael starts school, he and Dad will walk together every day, across the railway tracks to the outside world and I'll be left behind with my mother. She'll polish the dining room table in big, circular sweeps like she's seen on this TV show - *Clean Your Way to Fitness*. She'll make me hold my hands out with my thumbs stuck up while she makes a ball of her knitting wool. My hands will be tied.

I put the ketchup on the table.

"Why do our hands move Dad?"

Dad's newspaper remains steady but his navy eyes swivel up and peer at me over his glasses. "Because we tell them to," he says. "But I didn't tell my hands anything," I say, "and they put the ketchup down."

"You have a thing called The Brain," my dad tells me.

"SHE doesn't," Michael says. "She's a girl."

"The Brain orders your hands and your arms and your fingers and your toes to move. The Brain is like the General of the Army. He sends messages down little wires that work all the different parts of your body. It's like a puppet on strings."

"I'm going to learn about all this stuff at school," Michael boasts. "I'm going to know more than you. You get to learn everything at school. I'm going to learn how to read and write."

"I can write my name," I tell him. "Mam showed me."

He smiles. "Like spider's writing," he says. "Like a spider dipped its legs in ink and walked across the paper."

My mother plonks plates in front of Michael and my father. She grabs the ketchup bottle and holds it under the tap to wash it. "It's made a stain on the cloth," she says. "Didn't you see it was dirty, Claire? If you asked fewer questions you might see what was under your nose's end."

She takes me to the front garden to say goodbye. We are stuck behind the hedge while my father and brother walk away. She takes my hand from my mouth and waves it for me.

"Wish him luck," she says, and soon my hand waves by itself. My Brain sends a message down the wires and my teeth smile and my fingers wiggle.

"Good luck," I call. "Good luck."

My brother turns and smiles his smile at me.

"Wave till they reach the corner," my mother tells me, shaking my arm to speed it up. Wave till they're out of sight."

As she waves my right hand, my left hand does something of its own. The shaved privet is flat and bristly like Dad's face on Sundays. Most of the leaves are snipped across but I want a whole one, so my hand sneaks into the inside place where the shears never go. I find a round, undamaged leaf and pluck it. It is bad to pick things in the garden and to squash them. I have something private—a secret of my very own. I roll it between my fingers and its softness comforts me.

Michael and Dad turn and wave one last time before they turn the corner. It is my last chance before we go in to wash the dishes so I quickly look down at the leaf.

It is not a leaf but a big black spider.

The spider has a fat middle part and yellow stuff is coming out. It has little white things inside, like eggs. Some of its legs have come off, and though the rest still move, I know that the spider is dead. I have killed it. I wonder why my hand did that when my brain didn't tell it to.

Mam and Dad kill wasps together. Dad runs after them with a rolled-up newspaper.

"Not on the wallpaper!" my mother cries as she runs after him with a tea-spoon. "You'll make a mark. Wait till it lands on the window."

When the wasp lands on the window and buzzes and scrapes with its tiny feet trying to escape into the trees it can see outside, Dad bashes it and steps aside as it falls to the window sill. Mam runs in with the teaspoon while it's still stunned. She puts the handle where its head ties on and she pushes as the wasp wriggles and its stinging end curls around looking for the enemy. The head is tied on with such strong wires that she has to push and push.

"Take that!" Mam says as she crunches with the teaspoon and makes a face.

"Take that!" I whisper as I throw the spider down before my mother sees it. "Take that!"

I wipe the yellow stuff off my hand onto my cardigan and I never speak of it again.

—Robson (1996, *Privet*, 57-61)

Many contemporary cognitive scientists (Abram, 1996; Donald, 2001; Johnson, 2004) believe that our experience of consciousness is not purely located in the brain, as was commonly thought. Instead of seeing conscious-ness as only a set of neural firings in the cortex, they now believe that it is a cognitive network that extends beyond the brain through the body and even beyond as we perform and experience our identities through a complex cultural web that might include such things as our social networks and our sociopolitical contexts. For instance, my childish notions of gender were forged in the 1950s, with its veneration of the nuclear family tended by a "happy homemaker." The notion of a TV show called *Clean Your Way to*

Fitness raises a chuckle in the 21st century, but it was an actual show, and my mother actually watched it.

To frame identity this way, as a complex network that draws on information and energy beyond the brain, is to drive a stake into the heart of Cartesian dualism—the separation set between the mind, on one hand, and the body, on the other. In the Cartesian model, the human individual exists in isolation, and his or her consciousness is something that is separate from the consciousness of others. For the Cartesian philosopher, the self is interior, unknowable, discretely bounded. It is the vision conjured by my father in "Privet" (Robson, 1996)—in which the brain issues its commands through neural networks, like a lonely Wizard of Oz seated behind his curtain.

A more complex view of identity frames the self as fluid and performative, as it is conducted through sets of relationships among those things that have and continue to make up our life experiences. These include the natural and the man-made; the past, future, and current; the real and abstract; and the emotional, physical, spiritual, and intellectual. Identity becomes something created moment by moment rather than fixed, relational rather than individualistic, emotional and embodied rather than abstract and purely rational.

Needless to say, these two radically different orientations have led to equally different views of learning and education. In earlier Cartesian models of education, the mind is an empty vessel to be filled by knowledge. Students are schooled in rows. The teacher's job is to transmit knowledge and assess, through the testing of the measurable outcomes predicted by set curricula, how successfully students have absorbed the required information or learned to perform the required skills. Of course, although many contemporary educators have challenged this view of education, it is still alive and well. All too often, our school curriculum is limited to learning that can be quantified, delivered, and easily measured through the correct repetition of skills or the regurgitation of facts and information by individual students in tests. Learning that is messy, affective, or complex; learning that occurs in and through groups; or learning that feels and looks different for different students is often considered a less important by-product of "real" or "basic" education.

New theoretical perspectives of consciousness have implications for the field of education, generally, but also for the field of creative and autobiographical methods in the curriculum, also known as arts-based educational practices. It is to these that I now turn our attention.

Our human forebears understood the crucial power of text to both reflect and change our sense of reality, and for them, it was likely not a frill or a pastime but a tool in their survival, as they believed, for instance, that creating images of a successful hunt might lead to success in the hunt. In a way, we are just now catching up with our cave-painting ancestors, as we have begun to argue that making art is not just a form of decorative aesthetic expression, in which our outward reality is enhanced and improved by creative enterprises, but that it also changes both inner and outer realities. Grumet (1988) has written powerfully about the dangers of ignoring embodied aesthetic experiences, as the patriarchal curriculum severs mind from body, draining it of "the body's contributions to cognition, aesthetics, and community as realized through its capacity for sensuality, for movement, and for work" (p. 53). Many similar calls have been made for a more holistic, student-centered, process-driven, emergent approach to teaching and learning.

Seen this way, art is not just a way to reflect and represent what we see, to make a statement, or to entertain, although it can achieve all those purposes. With the great feminist scholar Frigga Haug (1992), I believe that art can also be a kind of detective work as it offers ways to better understand what we see and to change these understandings. In other words, I believe that making art can provide us with an education. Lewis (2000) has argued that consciousness both participates in acts of reading, writing, and imaging and, at the same time, is transformed by them. Acts of remembering or recollection are central to these creative processes. Like consciousness itself, memory is embodied, contextual, and distributed—it exists in and through our bodies as well in our "stuff." It resides in our scars and tattoos, our photograph albums, our china, our jewelry, and the stories we tell about ourselves and that others tell about us. Our memories are not fixed and determined but are capable of education.

This is not the time or place for a detailed exploration of the different kinds of memory that exist; however, a brief overview may be helpful. It is quite important, I feel, to acknowledge that "mapping the human brain" was considered possible at a time when scientists believed that such categories would be exhaustive and definitive. The categories of memory that I describe here are man-made constructs made differently by different theorists. I have considerably simplified their complex discussion in the interests of clarity and brevity, and I am aware, even as I set out the various categories, that these descriptions feel inadequate.

First, we are interested here in long-term memory rather than "short-term" or "sensory" memory. Short-term memory (sometimes called "working memory") is akin to a notepad on which we keep a few items of knowledge or information that we currently need. Sensory memory is our ability to re-call sensory experiences (such as touching an object), again for a short time. We are also not much concerned in this discussion with certain types of long-term memory, such as procedural memory (for instance, how to drive a car). This kind of memory usually does not require much effort of retrieval on our part but is implicit—"as easy," as we like to say, "as riding a bike." Our concern here is more with long-term declarative or explicit memory – that which must be consciously recalled. There are two main subsets of this category. The first is semantic memory—that which we know in terms of principles and facts, for instance, that Paris is the capital of France and that rivers flow down to the sea. We may not recall how we learned these facts, but we know them to be true.

The second category of long-term memory is more interesting in terms of our present discussion of recollection. Episodic memory, sometimes also called autobiographical memory, contains memories of particular life events (for instance, a first kiss or a birthday party) as they encapsulate the sensa-tions, emotions, and associations of a particular place or time, including the "what," the "when," and the "where." Visual memory, how things looked and were organized spatially, is an important subset of this category.

In any discussion of memory and identity, considering the notion of forgetting is important. Why do we remember some things and not others? Indeed, why do we notice some things and not others? Both perception and remembering are partial, in both senses of that word. We do not see everything because the act of perception occurs after acts of interpretation, a matter I will return to in Part III (see Chapter 7). We do not remember everything because to make sense of our lives and of the world, we need to filter what we choose to store in our long-term memories. Sometimes, these choices are simple—we might instantly delete what we paid for a pint of milk—but we might remember the person who took our money and made an interesting observation about the news for at least a little longer. These choices are driven by our identities and vice versa—someone careful about money might remember the cost of the milk and ignore the person who sold it to them.

Little is known about what happens when we "forget" something and, particularly, when, and how, we recall something we have "forgotten." One of today's well-known memory researchers, Elizabeth Loftus (1980), has identified four main reasons why we forget: retrieval failure, interference, failure to store, and motivated forgetting. *Retrieval failure* is a term that means that we cannot retrieve an item, although we know that it is something we once knew and might know again, for instance, the name of a person we had lunch with a week ago. The term is somewhat elliptical and self-referencing because it offers a description of forgetting rather than an explanation of why this might occur. Interference occurs when some more recent memory or information interferes with an older piece of knowledge or vice versa. For instance, if a friend changed her name, you might forget what you used to call her. Failure to store simply means that for some reason the information was not well encoded, usually because it was not considered important enough to commit to long-term memory. Motivated forgetting is more relevant to our discussion and is generally thought to take two forms: repression and suppression. It occurs when the events that have been repressed or suppressed are traumatic or disturbing, and it takes us into the unruly realm of the unconscious.

It is thought that we learn to repress or suppress painful memories as a protective mechanism. Trauma threatens the psyche and reduces our capacities to cope with everyday life as we become overwhelmed or paralyzed by grief, fear, or confusion. Most researchers in the field of cognition agree to the existence of implicit or unconscious memory in which these unwanted memories are stored, and they are getting close to understanding the chemical processes involved in suppression (Jovasevic et al., 2015). Jovasevic et al. also suggest that these memories can be retrieved and that such retrieval can be helpful in the formation of a healthy sense of self. When left unexamined, painful memories can lead (in the extreme) to anxiety, depression, and posttraumatic stress disorder. Anecdotal and research-based evidence from the fields of psychology, therapy, and (unless you are particularly blessed), your own life, also suggests that bringing difficult memories to the surface and processing them through the conscious mind can help us come to some better form of peace and emotional equilibrium. Oliver (2001, p. 10) defines this as "the Freudian notion of 'working through'" that which we find threatening in relation to otherness and difference.

I argue throughout this book that making art is one way, although not the only way, to engage in this work—work that is particularly important for those who have been oppressed, victimized, or marginalized, including those who identify as LGBTQ2sA+, and are statistically speaking more likely to have experienced abuse and trauma (Frederiksen-Goldsen et al., 2013).

Next, I turn to consider how this might operate on the ground. Although we now believe Freud was tragically misguided when it came to his approaches to the victims of trauma and abuse (almost all women), I believe that he has much to offer us when we think about methods of retrieving painful or difficult memories.

Freud (in Phillips, 2006) pays particular attention to what he calls screen memories: isolated recollections that feel significant to us, although their meaning is perplexing. On one hand, we remember such events because they were highly affective; on the other hand, we do not understand their significance because we have repressed them. Put another way, screen memories hint at something that is important, but they are not themselves that thing. As Freud puts it (rather beautifully), screen memories are valuable not because they are golden, but because "they have lain beside gold": "It is a case of displacement along the plane of association by contiguity," he notes, "the replacement of what is repressed by something in its spatial or temporal vicinity" (in Phillips, 2006, p. 545).

Screen memories, called lightbulb memories by some cognitive researchers, can serve as treasure maps for artists or, as Britzman (2006, p. 110) calls them, "placeholders for missed encounters." Once brought to the surface, they present strands that can be traced back to the psyche in associative processes. Freud's much-later essay, "The Magic Notepad" (in Phillips, 2006, originally published in 1925) raises the possibility that emotional stimuli continue to leave traces in the unconscious through adulthood and that the unconscious is capable of reproducing them from within, extending feelers toward the conscious mind. The unconscious, then, is capable of sending us hints, and these hints are associative. To quote Britzman (2006, p. 12) again, "making words from things has therapeutic action" as free association transports discourse into "the realm of the unapparent, the erased and the unnoticed."

As we turn to the short creative nonfiction piece that serves as an introduction to this chapter, we can see that it illustrates the argument presented in this first chapter. Because I wrote the piece, I can attest to the processes of its composition, as follows.

For many years, I experienced a recurring memory. I was small and in the garden of our early family home. I was absent-mindedly rolling what I thought was a leaf between my fingers, but when I looked down, I realized that it was a spider and that I had damaged it beyond repair. It was still alive but barely so. I was filled with a strange mix of emotions—horror, guilt, revulsion, and shame so strong that it still made me feel that I should not speak of the incident. The memory felt somewhat intrusive in this regard—unwanted and disturbing. That said, the memory was irritating rather than traumatic. Although it did pop into my consciousness unbidden from time to time, it did not keep me up at night, as they say, nor was it worthy of a therapy session. It was just something that had stuck, like a minor burr, in my psyche. It did not seem a worthy subject for a piece of writing, nor a fruitful one—after all, I could barely recall the incident, other than the details listed in this paragraph. The memory was temporally discrete and strictly bounded. I could not access what happened before or after the incident of the crushing. However, there the memory was—full of heat and energy. I decided to write about it, and this story was the product, written in one sitting, although edited later.

I will not co-opt the reader's role as receiver and interpreter of the text by an overly lengthy or exact analysis of "Privet" (Robson, 2006) except to say that it does accurately reflect some of the feelings experienced by my 6-year-old self. These included unexpressed jealousy and rage about my brother's ascendance, his freedom, and his access to intellectual life and close relationship with my father, as well as my feelings of conscription into the narrow and rigid world of domesticity represented and policed by my mother. Writing the story revealed important information to me about how I navigated and probably continue to navigate the difficulty of being a curious female in the patriarchy—at once angry and destructive and, at the same time, ashamed and horrified by the harm caused by my rage. I did not speak out or fight against the domestic structures that conscribed me. Instead, I hurt and destroyed something tiny, fragile, and innocent. Its death throes repulsed me and filled me with horror at my own misdirected anger.

I did not know these things before I wrote the piece, nor could I have accessed them without writing it. And these things about myself are true. And they are still true. The reader will have questions, I am sure. Did it happen the way I wrote? Probably not or, at least, not exactly. The story is about one aspect of my childhood. My fictionalized mother is more rigid; my brother, more smug; and my father, more distant than they "actually" were. I recall that I did wave good-bye to them every morning with my mother, but perhaps I did not do so on the morning in question. The details that describe the bungalow and its gardens are as exact as I can recall them; the conversations are invented, as are many of the other details, such as the Dr. Who pencil case. I will take up the business of "truth" later in the book, as I shall take up some of the practices that helped me in the writing of this piece, practices that serve this kind of memory work. For now, I will merely say that the experience of writing the piece was akin to "finding gold."

References

Abram, D. (1996). *The spell of the sensuous: Perception and language in a more-than-human world*. Teachers College Press.

Britzman, D. P. (2006). *Novel education: Psychoanalytic studies of learning and not learning* (Vol. 300). Peter Lang.

Donald, M. (2001). *A mind so rare: The evolution of human consciousness*. Norton.

Frederiksen-Goldsen, K. I., Kim, H-J., Barkan, S. E., Muraco, A., & Hoy-Ellis, C. P. (2013). Health disparities among lesbian, gay, and bisexual older adults: Results from a population-based study. *American Journal of Public Health, 103*(10), 1802–1809.

Grumet, M. (1988). *Bitter milk: Women and teaching*. University of Massachusetts Press.

Haug, F. (1992). *Beyond female masochism: Memory work and politics*. Verso.

Johnson, S. (2004). *Mind wide open: Your brain and the neuroscience of everyday life*. Scribner.

Jovasevic, V., Corcoran, K., Leaderbrand, K., Yamawaki, N., Guedea, A. L., Chen, H. J., Shepherd, G. M., & Radulovic, J. (2015). GABAergic mechanisms regulated by miR-33 encode state-dependent fear. *Nature Neuroscience, 18*, 1265–1271. https://doi.org/10.1038/nn.4084

Lewis, C. (2000). Limits of identification: The personal, pleasurable, and critical in reader response. *Journal of Literacy Research, 32*(2), 253–266.

Loftus, E. (1980). *Memory: Surprising insights into how we remember and why we forget*. Addison-Wesley.

Oliver, K. (2001). *Witnessing: beyond recognition*. University of Minnesota Press.

Phillips, A. (Ed.). (2006). The Penguin Freud reader. Penguin.

Robson, C. (1996). Privet. In R. Elwin (Ed.), *Countering the myths* (pp. 57–61). Women's Press.

CHAPTER TWO

Beyond Recognition

Figure 2.1: Memory Box by Judy Fletcher

In her book *Witnessing: Beyond Recognition*, Kelly Oliver (2001) acknowledges that human identity is constructed in response to the other but does not see why this should mean that human relationships are necessarily antagonistic and oppositional. She challenges the somewhat bleak view of human relationships adopted by critical theorists and poststructural thinkers such as Butler and Kristeva. Instead of seeing human beings as separated from the world and each other and communicating across an empty void, Oliver sees us as creatures who are naturally responsive, as we are connected by sensory networks that do not exist independently of each other but are subtly interconnected to form systems of sensation that operate through the entire body. Space is not empty but filled with forms of energy that connect us to the world and to each other. She further argues that to live in this state of "response-ability," as she calls it, carries with it an ethical and even biological imperative to relate and respond.

Oliver's (2001) arguments challenge the Cartesian view of isolated self and consciousness I questioned in Chapter 1 and then take things one step further. What would happen, Oliver asks, if we moved toward an ethic of *witnessing* oppression rather than just *recognizing* it? She argues that whereas oppression impacts the subjectivity of survivors to render them speechless and docile, bearing witness to the emotional reality of oppression offers the possibility of working through trauma to repair this damage. As she acknowledges the need for the experiences of survivors to be *recognized*, she suggests that subjectivity can be reconstituted when they bear *witness*, and she sets a crucial distinction between the two terms.

Recognition, Oliver (2001) argues, is about establishing the historical facts of what was seen, but bearing witness involves naming and acknowledging what cannot be seen so easily—the affective truth of one's experience within the sociopolitical context one inhabits. Witnessing, she suggests, is a way to restore visibility, agency, and voice to those whose subjectivity has been damaged by oppression. If those who have been rendered "other" can take back the ability to address and respond by taking a position as speaking subjects, then they rediscover what has been damaged—the roots of subjectivity, which Oliver defines as "address-bility," and "response-ability" (2001, p. 7). In doing so, they also rediscover connection and a sense of belonging, as they recover their sense of their own humanness, and see themselves reflected, loved, and appreciated rather than excluded, blamed, and alienated. Another way to put this might be to say that witnessing necessarily involves empathy.

This chapter then moves beyond the individual project of memory work offered in the previous chapter, as it offers one example of collective work that I believe answers Oliver's (2001) call for personal transformation through meaning-making and self-creation, or witnessing. This kind of reconstructive work is of particular importance in projects conducted with marginalized and oppressed populations, in my case, queer youth and elders, whose identities have historically been constructed around narratives of frailty and victimhood. To be fair, these narratives have some validity, in that research shows that both lesbian, gay, bisexual, transgender, and queer (LGBTQ) youth and elders are more "at risk" of such ills as suicide and depression (Frederiksen-Goldsen et al. 2013; Marshall, 2010). However, the participants I have worked with (both youth and elders) at once understand and reject the tropes of victimhood. They are realists, so they know that the statistics about such things as queer youth suicide help us get funding, but at the same time, they find these ideas of victimhood to be limiting, inaccurate, and demeaning—just another way that they can be marginalized.

The memory box shown in Figure 2.1 was made by Judy Fletcher (whose name is used at her request) as part of a group project I conducted with the members of an arts collective composed of people who self-define variously as lesbian, gay, bisexual, two spirit, asexual, and transsexual. They are all over the age of 60 and can thus be considered old. The group began under my direction as a writing group, in which people composed individual memoirs side by side, with myself as director and arbiter. Over the years, however, the group evolved into a more collaborative and less teacher-centered activist arts collective. Although work was still critiqued and revised, and there was always a focus on developing craft to communicate more effectively, there was an equal focus on collective listening, emotional support, risk-taking, and the development of theoretical political understandings and critiques. We worked in groups on various projects, and our activist agenda led us to experiment with different genres, including theater, three-dimensional art, and digital imagery. The fact that I was not an "expert" in these genres also necessarily led to a decentering of my pedagogies. Although I had extensive experience as a writing teacher, many members of the collective had a much greater understanding of some of the political and social issues we considered.

The Memory Project, during which the boxes were constructed, was funded by the federal government as part of my postdoctoral research into how collective arts engagements might support and investigate the ways in which individual and collective memories operate. Specifically, I wanted to see if working in a networked collective, rather than individually, might support the abilities of participants to recall and represent their life histories. In 2013, the first year of the project, participants talked together, shared texts they had found, and wrote individually about their memories for several months (under my direction). In the second year, each participant attempted to construct a memory box—a three-dimensional conceptual representation of a slice of individual memory. The entire collection of 20 boxes is viewable online at the group's website (www.quirk-e.com).

The box shown in Figure 2.1 was made by Judy Fletcher, whose real name is used at her request. Judy has been consulted in the process of writing this chapter and in the composition of all other publications that refer to her work (Robson, 2012; Robson & Sumara, 2016). She stands as an example of someone who has been marginalized and damaged by the processes of alienation that Oliver (2001) describes, since she has survived multiple forms of physical abuse and has worked with various therapists for many years to function well with her mental diagnoses. At the time of the project, Judy still occasionally coped with the strong feelings she experiences through acts of self-harm, and before joining this group, she was extremely isolated. In the early months and even years in which the group met, Judy rarely spoke in group settings. She was initially afraid to share her work because she felt that other group members would find its subject matter too difficult and distasteful. At the time the Memory Box Project began, Judy was much more comfortable in the group than she had been previously but was still shy, easily discouraged, and very disinclined to be in any way "on show."

The word Judy used to organize her box is *hiDdEn* (see Figure 2.1). The word is written, she said, "as if by a six-year-old who is just learning to write" (Journal entry, May 2013). Inside the box (see Figure 2.2), she offers the following definition of the word:

1. hiding—a beating, a whipping, a thrashing,

2. hidden—concealed, secret,

3. hide—the skin of an animal, either tanned or raw

A memorial plaque underneath reads "In memory of all the broken ones." Judy describes the box's interior as follows:

> There is a clear plastic box with three compartments. Inside, more leaves and potpourri and a dismembered girl doll. This is me! my head (with a large hole in the crown) is in one box; my body in another and my limbs are in the third. It is very difficult for the viewer to see these. It is always hard for people to see the brokenness of those who have learned to blend in. (Fletcher, my Shoebox, May 2013)

Sticking up out of the potpourri are plastic dolls' arms and legs, cobwebs, and splotches of bright red paint.

Figure 2.2: Inside Judy's Memory Box

Inside the box is an album of photographs, each of which shows a member of Judy's family staring directly at the camera (see Figures 2.3–2.8). The measuring chart behind them reminds us of police photographs, and their formal pose is organized by the gray and red lines at the bottom of each image and a surrounding thick black border. Each photograph includes a short statement inside a speech bubble.

Figure 2.3: Judy's Mother

Figure 2.4: Judy's Father

Figure 2.5: Judy's Older Sister

Figure 2.6: Judy's Brother

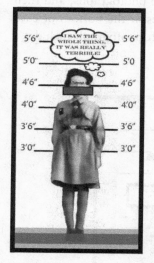

Figure 2.7: Judy's Younger Sister

Figure 2.8: Judy

Judy's mother wears a plain white housedress. Across her chest lies a black-bordered placard that reads "I can admit it now. I nearly killed you that day" (see Figure 2.3). Judy's father (Figure 2.4) stands "at ease" in a Royal Canadian Air Force uniform. His placard reads "Unfortunately, I was out of town a lot." His eyes are covered by a small blindfold. Judy's older sister (Figure 2.5) smiles and clasps her hands together in front of her in a gesture that is almost coquettish. She is dressed as if for a social occasion, in a short dress, tights, and a high-collared blouse. She wears a black blindfold like her father. Her thoughts float above her head in lacy, cloudlike speech bubbles. She says, "Probably I was out with my friends." The statement is conditional, tentative, and taken in the context of the image, it seems detached and uncaring.

Judy's brother (Figure 2.6) stands at attention in a Boy Scout uniform. Badges and epaulets gleam on his chest and shoulders, and he looks proud and happy. Like his sister, he seems not to remember much about "the incident," although, clearly, he is aware of it. He "guesses" that he was at school when it happened. Judy's younger sister (Figure 2.7) wears a Girl Guide uniform. The hem of her dress is crooked, the buckle of her belt is off-center, and her thick crepe stockings are creased. Her expression is difficult to read because her eyes are concealed behind spectacles and her mouth is covered by a red gag that obscures half her face. A large speech bubble sits squarely above her head, dominating the photograph. In large red capital letters, it reads "I saw the whole thing. It was really terrible."

The final photograph is of Judy (Figure 2.8). She is tiny—just over 4 feet tall—and wears a frilled white dress. There are ribbons in her hair. Her hands are held in front of her, and she seems to be holding something, perhaps a handkerchief. She has an air of childish delicacy and seems to be gazing at something or someone out of the shot. Unlike the rest of the family, she has stepped over the red line at the bottom of the image. Her face and much of her body are unevenly washed in red ink. A black uncompromising thought bubble floats above her head. It is some distance above it, perhaps to suggest dissociation or to emphasize her smallness. Childish handwritten letters in a mix of red capital and lowercase letters: "I thought I was going to die that day."

Initially, Judy felt overwhelmed by the task I had set the group. She saw the construction of a memory box as "just another thing [she] couldn't do" and considered paying lip service to it: "I thought that I would wait three months and then fill the box with Tinker Toys" (Fletcher, my Shoebox, May 2013). Soon after, however, she made the brave decision to work directly with a core issue: "I realized that feeling 'invisible' in the world had been a constant in my life. Maybe I could make that the 'theme' of the box" (Jounal entry, May 2013).

In her journaling and interviews about the process of making the box, Judy said that her mother spoke about the beating in later years but never addressed Judy directly or in a way that invited dialogue. As Judy put it, "she always said, 'I nearly killed *her* that day,' not 'I nearly killed *you* that day!' I was sitting right there but this was a shared memory of *theirs*."

This neatly illustrates the point Oliver (2001) makes about the ways in which oppression directly attacks and attempts to destroy the subjectivity of the victim. In making the box, Judy decided to "work through" this victimization to reclaim her identity. There were quite a number of "firsts" for Judy in the process. Not only did she use actual photographs of her family members, but she also used a photograph of herself—the first time ever that she has represented herself in her work other than as a stick figure. Judy also decided to include her box in all public exhibitions of the Memory Box Collection, an act of self-revelation that would have been impossible for her in previous years. Finally, Judy became a valued consultant in the group as many turned to her for advice and practical help in making their own boxes. Her confidence grew, and she began to form strong connections with others in the group, particularly, two of the men.

Judy's box can be read as a form of testimony or witnessing, as it steps the viewer through the brutal event it depicts. On several occasions, I have watched strangers pick up the box somewhat casually, linger, understand, and be overwhelmed by its contents (most end up in tears). Judy not only recognizes the incident—a small child being beaten by someone responsible for her care and safety—but she also invites us to witness its emotional force. She communicates how she was psychically pulled apart and broken and shows graphically how most of her family, those she solely depended on for acknowledgment, chose not to see what had happened.

In making and showing the box, Judy came to see herself as a warrior rather than a victim. She reclaimed the memory that at once terrorized her and silenced her ability to speak of that terror. Her family claimed the memory and denied her right to it, but after making the box, she said, "I am going to take it back. It is *my* memory now!" This reclaiming allowed her to see herself as a witness, speaking up for "all the broken ones." Here's Judy again, as she writes about this reclaiming in her journal:

I decided that I didn't want to be too specific after all. I did not want to demonstrate a savage beating on a particular child. In fact, I wanted it to remind people that terrible things are done to children and most families claim it as "none of the outside world's business." (May 2013)

Judy's testimony is produced through an individual act of great courage; it is also the product of the collective in which it occurred, and significantly, it was designed for an audience. Although Judy was somewhat apprehensive at the beginning of the project, she drew comfort from the fact that the rest of the group were committed to the same task. "I would not have thought of doing this on my own," she said in an interview, "and I probably would not have stuck with it if I did" (Interview, June, 2013). She could also practice disclosure in the group by showing the box to a few members she trusted there before sending it out to be seen by strangers. Their responses surprised her: "I did not realize how much stored up emotion I was putting into the box until I showed the finished shoebox to someone" (Journal entry, May, 2013). Such responses, as we know, also serve to validate and support the damaged subjectivity of those who have suffered violence at the hands of others.

Judy would have been unlikely to discuss what happened to her in public or even share it with the members of her arts collective, but came to feel that the process of working with a difficult memory through art making was possible and even enjoyable. As the box developed, it provided a productive third space in which Judy worked at a pace that felt safe. "The Process surprised me. It was slow but almost every day I thought of a small detail that could be added" (Journal entry, May 2013). Rather than trying to address the incident head-on, say, through writing directly about it or describing it to someone else, it seemed that Judy was able to approach it bit by bit, tangentially and without disclosing the process to others. The practical challenges of making of the box were a "distraction," Judy said (Interview, June, 2013) as she focused on "trying to figure out how to get the paper here and how to get the stuff stable in the box." For sure, there were times that the process was emotionally difficult. For instance, "it turned out to be difficult to tear [the doll] apart. . . . I was taking a hacksaw to a little doll who I knew was me" (Interview, June, 2013).

Through her memory box, Judy's core message to her audience is that "it is always hard for people to see the brokenness of those who have learned to blend in" (Journal entry, May, 2013). Her work points to a key dilemma for many of us who identify as queer. We want to pass, to be accepted for our simple humanity, and at the same time, we know how important it is to speak up about injustice. Judy's box encapsulates the tension that that many of us have felt throughout our lives—particularly the young and the old—between being boxed in by the gloomy narratives that others tell about us, on one hand, and being exposed to criticism and even violence if we tell our own stories. As Oliver (2001) points out, when the audience's gaze involves examination and objectification, recognition "either returns us to the recognition of sameness or becomes misrecognition that leads to hostility" (p. 11). In this work, Judy moved beyond her individual experience of abuse to speak for all the broken ones. She bears witness to what is beyond recognition.

References

Frederiksen-Goldsen, K.I., Kim, H-J., Barkan, S.E., Muraco, A., & Hoy-Ellis, C.P. (2013). Health disparities among lesbian, gay, and bisexual older adults: Results from a population-based study. *American Journal of Public Health, 103*(10), 1802–1809.

Marshall, D. (2010). Popular culture, the 'victim' trope and queer youth analytics. *International Journal of Qualitative Studies in Education, 23*(1), 65–85. doi:10.1080/09518390903447176

Oliver, K. (2001). *Witnessing: beyond recognition*. University of Minnesota Press.

Robson, C. (2012). *Writing for change: Research as public pedagogy and arts-based activism*. Peter Lang.

Robson, C., & Sumara, D. (2016). In memory of all the broken ones: Catalytic validity through critical arts research for social change. *International Journal of Qualitative Studies in Education, 29*(5), 617–639. http://dx.doi.org/10.1080/09518398.2016.1139211

CHAPTER THREE

Fishing for Difference

Dusk was waiting in the wings. The reflection of the boat ran along beside them trying to keep up, never getting ahead. The water shimmered as the last rays of the sun tried to penetrate the depths. The surface of the water was becoming busy. Hundreds of tiny flies covered the water like a knotted comforter.

—Morrissey (2009, p. 3)

IN THIS CHAPTER, I argue that when we frame memory as a process of complex recollection rather than one of simple recall, we are able to open spaces for reflection so that we are not only able to remember more but to remember it differently and with greater resonance as well. Seen this way, remembering becomes a process of "re-collection" of all those items that composed and situated the original experience, including the affective and sociopolitical context in which it occurred. Cvetkovich (2003) calls these recollections and representations "archives of feeling" as she suggests that once constructed, these archives can serve as records of experiences that have often been overlooked in mainstream culture. Here, I argue that they also help us on an individual level as we assemble and reassemble our memories and identities, which are not fixed but constantly negotiable.

Of course, telling stories does not always result in greater insight. Indeed, it can do the opposite, by inviting us to reinscribe narratives and embed them more deeply in our psyches. Oral historian Sandro Portelli (1981) calls such stories "epic narratives" as he suggests that, like epics of all kinds, they strive for heightened tone and drama. The following is an example drawn from the work of lesbian activist Chris Morrissey (whose work is also quoted in the chapter-opening epigraph). It describes a moment of triumph in Chris and her partner's struggle to change the law around immigration for same-sex couples:

Hundreds of people are gathered under the glass roof of the Law Courts. Bridget and I are walking toward the stage. We are grinning from ear to ear. We have overcome the last hurdle. We are handed a trophy. It is shaped like a house. We enter and we know it is home. We know we have come home. (Morrissey, 2008, p. 1)

Although this was indeed an epic event, well worthy of public record, this particular extract does not do it full justice or, at the very least, is not written with the same eye for detail as the first extract, written a year later. Chris uses imagery to convey the affective impact of their victory—"grinning from ear to ear," "overcoming the last hurdle"—but both images are somewhat tired from overuse. The image of the trophy, in the form of a house, is ingenious but is not unpacked sufficiently to have the impact Chris hoped for here. The short sentences strive for drama but end up sounding repetitive.

In the previous chapter, I talked about the narcissism of minor differences (Freud, 1929) and their particular importance for those who identify as queer. For the queer subject, standing out can be physically and psychically dangerous, even as speaking up can repair damaged subjectivity. Here, I look at this topic from another angle, as I consider how queer culture has generated its own normative and essentializing epic narratives, which can obscure more complex ones. Paradoxically, the queer subject tends to cling tenaciously to intelligible gay/lesbian narrative structures. When interviewed, lesbian, gay, transgender, and queer (LGBTQ) participants often revert to the classic queer epic narrative—the pervasive coming-out story (Boyd, 2008), whatever the topic under discussion. As Boyd (2008) tried to interview gay participants about their relationship to San Francisco, for instance, they inexorably steered the conversation back to their first same-sex relationship. Boyd's narrators knew that they had been selected because they were gay; therefore, they felt that this is what made them worthy of representation. Second, as Thompson (2009, p. 167) has pointed out, "memories which are discreditable, or positively dangerous, are most likely to be quietly buried." This is especially true of respondents who feel that they live under threat, such as gay and lesbian narrators (Boyd, 2008). In this way, LGBTQ accounts can serve normalize their own experiences in their own ways.

Haug (1992) believes that writers must be taught how to *investigate* and *revise* first-draft narratives rather than just to reinscribe them. It is, she thinks, a special kind of detective work that requires certain skills and methods of work. I would add that this kind of work, which Haug calls a language school, is particularly necessary for queer people, for the reasons I have given earlier. In 2007, I created a kind of language school for six lesbian elders to see what might happen as they helped each other dig below the surface of their comfortable narratives (Robson, 2012). We met together for two years, at a lesbian-owned and -operated restaurant on the Eastside of Vancouver, British Columbia, Canada. The research was funded by the Social Science and Humanities Research Council of Canada.

I chose to work with lesbian seniors because they have lived through times of great change in terms of cultural and societal attitudes and legal changes regarding LGBTQ rights (Stein, 1997). In this way, their histories are *overdetermined* in that they are packed with cultural assumptions, the impact of developments in queer and feminist theory, and the social conditions and mores of lesbian culture. Boyd (2008, p. 180) has pointed out that queer identities are "constructed around very limited sets of meaning," and these meanings change with time, much more so than in heterosexual life. It is difficult, for instance, to talk or write about what it was like in the past, say, in butch/femme bar culture, in a world in which moral frameworks have changed so radically since the 1950s (Chenier, 2004). Being butch in the 1950s was to stand out in ways that are barely conceivable in the 2020s.

However, lesbian lives are also *undetermined* in that the experiences of older lesbians are rarely represented in the media, or in literary and historical accounts, and when they are represented, they tend to essentialize both the categories of *old* and *lesbian*. For instance, the women and I reread two lesbian classics: *The Well of Loneliness* (Hall, 1928) and *Rubyfruit Jungle* (Brown, 1977). Reading the two texts against each other was interesting. On one hand, we found the former to be terribly depressing and the latter to be unrealistic in its celebratory "single story." At that time, we could find no texts that offered nuanced and realistic representations of lesbian culture and none that depicted older lesbians. In a way, our work together was an exploration of this space between queer optimism and queer pessimism.

I led the group in a 2-year experiment with critical literary life writing and participated in all the writing exercises I set. Our work together included close reading and analyses of literary texts (their own and that of others). Although we were disappointed by the paucity of robust lesbian memoirs, we read, and very much enjoyed, White's (2000) autobiographic novel, *A Boy's Own Story*, for its frankness, its portrayals of fallibility, and its closely written imagery and descriptions. I encouraged the group to begin experimenting with these in their work, allowing it to open up to new possibilities. We experimented with writing in various genres (including rants and parables), and we imitated sections of writing from the texts we read. In the second year of the project, all the women completed what they liked to call a *memoirette*. They worked to achieve a tight thematic focus rather than attempting to cover their entire lives chronologically.

As already mentioned, the two short extracts reproduced in this chapter were written by the same author, Chris Morrissey, a woman who is quite literally, a poster child for lesbian activism (see Figure 3.1). Chris stands out in many ways. Raised in a Catholic family, she became a nun in her late teens, fell in love with another nun, and quit the church. On their arrival in Canada, her partner, Bridget, was denied residency, so Chris issued a legal challenge to the Supreme Court of Canada about its homophobic immigration laws and won her case, thus changing the lives of many other same-sex couples. She went on to found Rainbow Refugees, an organization that has rightly brought her into the spotlight of public attention. In 2011, she was voted one of 12 "Remarkable Women of Vancouver" (see Figure 3.1). She has also received the Queen's Jubilee Medal and just recently, in 2020, Canada's highest accolade, the Order of Canada.

The working title for Chris's memoirette was "*A Problem With Authority*," and in her initial plan, she aimed to trace the history of her oppression by a domineering father and by the monolithic Catholic Church. She learned to identify and dramatize scenes that crystallized this systematic and systemic oppression, which culminated in her father seeing her off to a convent with the admonishment that "he that puts his hand to the plow and looks back is not worthy of the kingdom of God" and on to the Mother Superior, who moved Morrissey to another convent because she had developed a "particular friendship" with another woman.

As Chris began unpacking these scenes, however, she began to notice (with the help of the group) that despite living within rigid social structures for much of her childhood and youth, she had developed strategies of what we might call everyday resistance to everyday trauma. Although outright rebellion was not an option when she was a child, Morrissey perfected a kind of guerilla insolence, skirting the very edges of her father's rules and employing a quiet stubbornness, for instance, by refusing to speak to any-

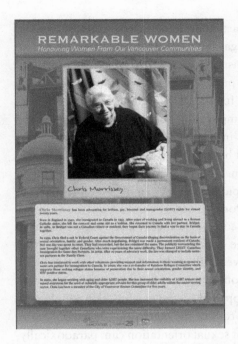

Figure 3.1: Chris Morrissey, Remarkable Woman of Vancouver

one in the family for three whole days. She continued this subversive activity as a nun, as she sabotaged the priests' ironing, slipped under the mosquito net of another nun's bed at night, and saw to it that she and her lover were shipped off to the same location in Chile, without revealing their "special friendship." Once there, she applied her covert tactics to the broader politics of resistance, carrying messages for anti-Pinochet resistance fighters in her burlap standard-issue nun bag and organizing in secret with local women.

As she wrote her memoirette, Chris became aware of a new through line—one about courage and agency rather than the "female masochism" that Haug (1992) suggests so many women's stories, such as *The Well of Loneliness* (Hall, 1928). By the end of the project, Chris had retitled her memoir as *A Problem For Authority* rather than *A Problem With Authority*. In writing about her life, she discovered that far from being just a victim, she was a protagonist who had developed robust means of resistance and employed them to great effect.

This was the first outcome of Chris's work in the group, but at the very end of our 2-year journey, she took a further step. Many of the stories she had written up to this point had a particular didactic aim. Chris wanted to record experiences that might raise gay and lesbian political visibility and record key advances in queer social history and in Latin American resistance to dictatorship. It was a worthwhile project. Alternative epic narratives are a vital way to set the record straight for the individual and for the community. This one certainly marks an important moment in Morrissey's and Bridget's lives and a triumph for gay immigration rights in Canada. Chris's memoirette, yet to be published, will be a wonderful addition to the historical record, and it will be well written.

However, as I have suggested, epic narratives can also tend to obscure more subtle and surprising stories. Portelli (1981) shows how they can become so fixed, especially for older people (Thompson, 2009, p. 184), that they "arrest consciousness." It can be difficult to get such narrators to talk about anything else or to see the events they describe in any other way. Above all, their celebratory, heroic tone can preclude emotional nuances—the complexities of what actually happened on the ground. For people who identify as queer, such stories can reproduce the conditions of fixed identity formations. The "minor difference" of sexual orientation can, paradoxically, obscure other important minor differences—experiences and identifications that have nothing to do with sexuality or represent sexuality as complex, difficult, or disturbing. As Chimamanda (TED, 2009) has eloquently put it, the danger of a single story is that it creates stereotypes that are not necessarily *untrue* but *incomplete*.

The second extract that opens this discussion is from Morrissey's short prose memoir *Fishing*, about a day spent on the water with her father on their annual family holiday at Bednesti Lake. There is a moment that Morrissey perceives as significant, although she did not quite understand why. It is a moment in which nothing much happens, but a lot is going on.

As I compare this to the earlier extract of Morrissey's work, I note the sophistication and originality of the imagery (similar to White's, 2000, work), which successfully communicates a sense of immanence and energy: the boat's reflection strives to catch up with the action, the sun tries to penetrate the surface of the water, and the flies gather in their hundreds "like a knotted comforter." Although the young protagonist does eventually catch a fish (which gets away), Chris said that this was not really the central event. She was trying to capture something else: an elusive feeling she had that day just before the fish was caught. She was unable, in our conversation about this piece, to put her finger on exactly what this was, but she knew that it was to do with the word *shimmering* and the quiet beauty of the lake. It was also to do with sharing this time with her father, a man who did not normally pay her any attention. For Chris as an individual, this move toward understanding the bond between her and her father, however tenuous, was surprising and personally important.

Zwicky (2006, p. 95) argues that lyric's intuition is to reach beyond and behind what she calls the "grammars of consequence" to find "resonance," following trails of imagery and association that may lead us into surprising points of departure from epic narratives that we have told and retold. Lyric thus becomes the genre of choice for the astonished treatment of memory and, in particular, for the memory of experiences that fall outside the pale of communal mythmaking. Whereas autobiography takes a linear and sensible approach to narrative, critical life writing can take us beyond the pale and past the predictable single story. It has the ability to engage authors in a search for subtle themes and meanings and for finer distinctions. These are distinctions that Jane Austen, writing at the end of the seventeenth century, would have called "nice"—perceptions and responses that make up sensibility rather than sense and meaning rather than simple representational chronology.

Chris Morrissey's move from *with* to *for* in her title does not so much demonstrate increased agency—she has developed this in spades during her long activist life—but rather an increased ability to reanalyze her past in the light of current circumstances and insights. I also believe that this work made us all think harder about the ways in which discourses developed to support minor differences can become marginalizing in themselves. The states of being old and being queer are both over- and underdetermined, both packed with emotional charge and yet not represented in mainstream culture with a wide degree of subtlety or range of interpretation. Firsthand accounts such as Chris's can complicate such normalizing and restrictive narratives.

All we have to go on as we remember, revise, and represent our histories and identities are acts of remembering and forgetting. However, this is true for all history, as even "matters of record" began with lived experience. Their retelling has been influenced by interpretation, the forces of trauma, repression, and cultural assumptions. In this first section of the book, I have offered some ways to begin the creative exploration of memories, to move them into productive witnessing and beyond predictable epic narratives into more complicated and nuanced recollections of what happened.

In the next section, I go on to consider what happens when we do this work successfully, to enter what Britzman (2006, p. 12) calls the realm of "the unapparent, the erased, the unrecognized, and the things one did not mean to say." This is dangerous territory, and as Freud (1929) has pointed out, the uncanniest things to emerge are often those that are somehow most familiar. As well as acknowledging the process of suppression and resistance to these insights, I offer some methods for navigating the difficulties of recognition.

References

Boyd, N. A. (2008). Who is the subject? Queer theory meets oral history. *Journal of the History of Sexuality, 17*(2), 177–189.

Britzman, D. P. (2006). *Novel education: Psychoanalytic studies of learning and not learning* (Vol. 300). Peter Lang.

Brown, R. M. (1977). *Rubyfruit jungle*. Bantam Books.

Chenier, E. (2004). Rethinking class in lesbian bar culture: Living 'the gay life' in Toronto, 1955–1965. *Left History, 9*(2), 85–118.

Cvetkovich, A. (2003). *An archive of feelings: Trauma, sexuality, and lesbian public cultures*. Duke University Press.

Freud, S. (1929). *Civilization and its discontents*. Pelican.

Hall, R. (1928). *The well of loneliness*. Jonathan Cape.

Haug, F. (1992). *Beyond female masochism: Memory work and politics*. Verso.

Morrissey, C. (2008). *Home*. Unpublished short story.

Morrissey, C. (2009). *Fishing*. Unpublished short story.

Portelli, A. (1981). The peculiarities of oral history. *Journal of the Canadian Association for Curriculum Studies, 2*(1), 96–107.

Robson, C. (2012). *Writing for change: Research as public pedagogy and arts-based activism*. Peter Lang.

Stein, A. (1997). *Sex and sensibility: Stories of a lesbian generation*. University of California Press.

TED. (2009, October 7). *The danger of a single story: Chimamanda Ngozi Adichie* [Video]. YouTube. http://www.youtube.com/watch?v=D9Ihs241zeg

Thompson, P. (2009) *The voice of the past: Oral history*. Oxford University Press.

White, E. (2000). *A boy's own story*. Vintage.

Zwicky, J. (2006). In R. Finley, P. Friesen, A. Hunter, A. Simpson, & J. Zwicky (Eds.), *A ragged pen: Essays on poetry and memory*. Gaspereau Press, 87-105.

PART II

RECOGNIZING

CHAPTER FOUR

Resistance and Motivated Forgetting

It's a snapping turtle that pushes me out of it. She's an old one, who belongs here more than I do, but I've invaded her space. I see her heading up from the depths—aiming right for me, head up and out, long legs grabbing the water, shell flaring up around her.

That fast, I care.

Can I out swim an angry turtle? On land, she's awkward. In the water, she's graceful, poised, not an awkward bone in her body. Each movement propels her to exactly where she wants to be. And she's fast. Does she know there's a difference, or is it instinct only?

I swim. For my life, it feels. And in some way, it is.

—Val Innes

In Chapter 3, I argue that when we do our memory work well, we enter what Britzman (2006, p. 12) calls the realm of "the unapparent, the erased, the unrecognized, and the things one did not mean to say." In this next section, I consider the uneasy business of entering this strange realm, essentially a process of recognition or re-recognition, especially for individuals who identify as queer because deviation from cultural norms and consequent trauma can open up, close down, delay, or accelerate the impact of experiences and thus the ways in which they are remembered (Ahmed, 2010; Berlant, 2010; Massumi, 2010). I am suggesting that there is such a thing as "queer memory" and that it operates differently from heterosexual memory.

In his essay on the uncanny, Freud (1919) argues that to experience the uncanny or the unrecognized, is in a sense, its own opposite in that the uncanny proceeds from something familiar that has been repressed. The literature on trauma is clear that such repression is often the direct result of oppression, victimization, and violence, which render some memories difficult or even impossible to access (Britzman, 2006; Felman & Laub, 1992). It is also generally acknowledged that queer individuals experience more trauma than their heterosexual counterparts (D'Augelli & Grossman, 2001; Haas et al., 2011) and are also subject to quotidian slights and injuries generated by homophobia and misogyny, which Cvetkovich (1995) has termed "everyday" or "insidious" trauma. In this way, their memories are more likely to have been impacted by repression.

Many of the queer writers I have worked with believe this to be true, and they describe these effects as cumulative as they point out that they have lived through a historic period when queer people were locked up, rejected by their families, denied access to their children or grandchildren, and subjected to "cures," including electric shock and aversion therapies—something that happened to a close friend of Val's, whose work forms the basis of this chapter. It is worth noting here that lesbian women tend to be less visible and less wealthy than gay men, and they also encounter the heightened misogyny that faces women who choose to reject sexual, financial, and emotional dependency on men, thus challenging patriarchal constructions of male dominance and notions of what constitutes "normal" sexual behaviors (Sumara, 2008).

Many of my queer research participants reported experiencing forgetfulness when it comes to difficult memories—a phenomenon that is called motivated forgetting (Rubin, in Roediger et al., 2007). One participant, a gay man called Douglas, put it this way: "I mean my memory is the shits. The first thing I think of [is that] I just forget everything. That is the first thing I think of when I hear the word 'memory.'" Val also referred to her forgetfulness frequently during interviews and discussions:

I've never written about that time actually. A lot of it's a blur, so I think it was an absolutely life forming experience for me, and one that I've never really dealt with. (Discussion 6)

I found this [piece of writing] extraordinarily difficult to do. In fact, I wrote two of them and it was like I was working through a fog. I obviously protected myself from this period in my life so I'm not sure that I wasn't even guessing when I wrote this. (Discussion 7)

It's really elusive and so unless I write it down, I have little access to it. (Discussion 7)

Going back to Freud's (1919) notion of the uncanny, it is also worth noting that Val's struggle to recall the traumatic life events of that time (a bad breakup) is captured in the allusive image of the turtle: the feeling that something old, familiar, and dangerous is attempting to surface from the murky depths of the lake. I argue here that motivated forgetting is not so much a biological or cognitive issue as a sociological or affective one.

Gee (in Luria et al., 2006) sets a distinction between *acquisition* and *learning*. He argues that the unreflective citizen *acquires* learning, as something given or handed down, whereas the activated, critical subject *learns*, by observing and critiquing that which is usually taken as read. This is true of our gender and sexual identifications. Freud (in Phillips, 2006) has famously said that children are "polymorphously perverse" in that they have not yet become subject to cultural conditioning or taboos. This implies that that "standards of 'normal' gender and sexuality are not rooted in some essence of the self" but rather learned behaviors (Dimock, 2012, para 4). People assemble the data of their own lives in such a way that they can live with themselves in noncontradictory ways. In this chapter, I argue that for the queer author and the female author, these processes of assembly can be more challenging as we exist in a state of cultural disjuncture.

The through lines we assemble are strongly influenced by cultural scripts (Moon, 2006). Enshrined in popular culture, such as books, films, and advertising, these scripts (in the Western world at least) trace a heterosexual trajectory from childhood, through adolescence, first kiss, courtship, marriage, career, retirement, and on into grandparenting and old age. These acquired practices of the day are instinctive and almost unnoticeable—we are just following the script. Whereas the acquired practices of the day become instinctive, learning is noticeable; it produces conscious knowledge through analysis. To pursue my analogy further, those of us who identify as homosexual, bisexual, asexual, or trans* find that we have to invent our own scripts. Of course, many heterosexual people ("single mothers," "widowers," "divorcees," or "spinsters") refuse or fail to conform to dominant scripts, and some lesbian, gay, bisexual, transgender, and queer (LGBTQ) individuals adhere to them. Nonetheless, they still serve as organizing narratives that largely exclude homosexuals. As Ahmed (2010, p. 91) has put it, "queer and feminist histories are the histories of those who are willing to risk the consequences of deviation."

The epigraph opening this chapter is from a piece of writing by Val Innes, composed during the same research project with old lesbian activists that I drew on in Chapter 3. It can be said to crystallize her intellectual journey in the group with reflections about speech and silence—a topic that resonated with other members of this group of lesbians. Val's writing about the ancient turtle—comfortable in her own skin, clear in her intention, beautiful and yet dangerous—reads like a message from the depths of the unconscious to a narrator who is unclear, uncertain, and literally out of her element at the moment of the encounter.

Val's memoir journey began when we discussed our first common text, Carol Shields's (2002) novel *Unless*. Val questioned the credibility of one of the characters, Norah, who sits on a street corner in silence, holding a sign that says, simply, "Goodness." Val liked the book on the whole but was extremely irritated by Norah's insistence on silence. "What the hell would sitting on a street corner do?" she asked the rest of the group (Robson & Sumara, 2007–2009, p. 72). Her responses were so visceral that I encouraged her to dig into them as she wrote. As Val explored her own history with speech and silence, she began to fit things together differently.

Val used the writing exercises I set to think about her own journey with speech and silence. She recalled that after an angry husband threatened her with a lawsuit (after learning of Val's affair with his wife) when she was in her 20s, she "went into a shell," telling herself "I'll have a career. I just won't have a personal life" (Robson & Sumara, 2007–2009, p. 72). Some years later, Val did enter another relationship, this time with a very out lesbian, who ended things because Val "was in six double locked closets" (Robson & Sumara, 2007–2009, p. 73). These difficult sexual experiences, in which neither silence nor speech seemed to work, were lived against the backdrop of a family that seemed to embrace heteronormative discourse quite uncritically. "It was an upbringing," Val wrote, consisting of "an inability to think outside the box" (Robson & Sumara, 2007–2009, p. 73).

Ironically, Val was never sure whether her parents disapproved of homosexuality precisely because it was never discussed. Although she seemed to recall that her father might have "put down male gays" (Robson & Sumara, 2007–2009, p. 73), she was not sure that he had done so, and she could not recall what her parents had thought about lesbians, if anything. In this way, we see that recognition of her sexual identity, for Val, was foreclosed by acceptance of cultural norms and scripts, which seemed to preclude the need to even begin to discuss them. Val's writing during our project suggests that the ways in which LGBTQ individuals remember and describe their life experiences are affected by disjuncture, motivated forgetting, self-inflicted silence, and unexamined assumptions—a hypothesis supported by the literature on depression (Cvetkovich, 2012) and melancholy (Butler, 1997).

It was only after a friend talked her out of suicide that Val finally came out to her father. It was a difficult moment. Val's father was a doctor, and homosexuality was still seen as an illness at that time. One of Val's own friends had been taken out of college to be given electric shock treatments. As she told the story, Val recalled the exact words she used to break the news—an eerie ventriloquism of the response she expected. Her opening words frame her sexuality as pathological: "Dad, I think I'm sick. . . . I think I'm gay, Dad. I'm so unhappy; I think it'd be easier if I just died."

At this point, Val's narrative takes an unexpected turn. Instead of being angry, her father embraced her. According to Val, he "changed from 'gays are bad,' to 'gays are fine'" (Robson & Sumara, 2007–2009, p. 73). Val told her mother, who also accepted her sexual identity (to the point of taking care of some of Val's lesbian friends who had been rejected by their families). Val insisted on finding a therapist who was not homophobic, and as breaking silence opened up new channels of communication, Val noted that the entire family became closer and more openly loving (Robson & Sumara, 2007–2009, p. 73): "My family didn't hug until I came out."

All too often, gay and lesbian fiction posits coming out as a single story (see TED, 2009), which ends in sexual bliss and individual agency (albeit after family disapproval). One of the narratives that Val very much liked during our research was the iconic lesbian novel *Rubyfruit Jungle* (Brown, 1977), one of the texts we read as part of our work together. Its lesbian protagonist, Molly, maintains an indomitable cheerfulness in the face of all adversity, including the worst kind of homophobia. She is impervious to psychic harm and seems completely inured to doubt or confusion about her sexual choices. Val's own early writing was equally celebratory and uncomplicated; for instance, she described her first visit to a lesbian dance, after which she "never looked back." This is a story often told by lesbian writers—a kind of antidote to the depressing conclusion of *The Well of Loneliness* (Hall, 1981), which we also read in the group (and Val very much disliked). All cultures, even countercultures, develop their own normative discourses, and the uncomplicated coming-out story, after which one "never looks back," is a favorite.

Less often told are more complex stories—about not coming out or the more disturbing nuances of coming out, such as internalized homophobia and subtler forms of rejection. Again, much has been written about overt homophobia and transphobia, but less attention has been given to the ways in which heteronormativity limits understanding and learning *before* the act of conscious reflection. Yet for older lesbians who lived in times of greater social oppression, these experiences are much more typical.

Writing the seemingly inconsequential piece about the turtle proved to be a turning point for Val. She puzzled over the piece—particularly the last line ("I swim. For my life, it feels. And in some way, it is"). "What does that even mean?" she asked (personal communication, April 10, 2013). For Val, it became a core story, even though she did not consciously understand its significance, she knew that her turtle had considerable resonance. As Freud might have put it, it "had lain by gold."

Val's curiosity fueled continued work with the memories she had uncovered, and as a consequence, she discovered a more complicated and less celebratory narrative. She began to wonder if she had just invented her parents' disapproval in the face of their silence? Had she put herself through so much agony for nothing? In her later writing, she uncovered a terrible irony at the heart of her story: a self-inflicted silence that is only too familiar for many queer people. As she wrote about her ongoing phobia of speaking in public and her failure to come out as a university professor, she was somewhat shocked to realize that the phobia about public speaking began shortly after her mother's death. Although her mother had been very accepting in those final years before her death and had a severe heart condition (which put her life in jeopardy), Val recalled her father having once told her that upsetting her mother might kill her, and she wondered if, even subconsciously, she had connected the act of speaking and her mother's death, and had opted for silence. "Did I take my voice away for ten years?" (Robson & Sumara, 2007–2009, p. 29), she asked the group. In the same transcript, she reports on a recent failure to respond to homophobic comments from students in a class that she was teaching: "And I'm sitting there," she told us, "thinking, 'You need to say something. You need to say something. You need to say something.' And I didn't." The effects of homophobia continue to haunt the pond long after the act of coming out and even after the fact of acceptance.

Identity, and, by extension, our sense of reality, is "routinely created and sustained in the actions of the individual" (Giddens, 1991, p. 52), and there is general agreement that our sense of continuous and coherent self depends upon our ability to put these actions and events into a chronological narrative, or story (Sutton, 2012). In a novel, these fictitious events might be called plot points, and taken together, they build a plot or through line. Because our memories are necessarily selective, we remember certain events and forget others as we make choices about what is perceived as being significant. Typically, the moments we remember are those that affected us profoundly or those that we consider to be culturally important (Pillemer et al. 1998). We argue here that for queer individuals, these important moments (which I call "bookmarks") may be differently assembled. Linear narratives may be drastically interrupted.

As Massumi (2010, p. 9) has written, "all that a self-creating occasion of experience ultimately 'knows' of the world's activity is how it has taken up a portion of it into its own becoming. 'What' this will have been exactly retains a certain indeterminacy as long as the becoming is still in process, so that the 'what' of an experience is only fully definite at its culmination." In the same vein, Caruth (1996, p. 5) has argued that "the greatest confrontation with reality may also occur as an absolute numbing to it," and "immediacy, paradoxically enough, may take the form of belatedness." Trauma may not only cause us to forget traumatic events, but it may also prevent us from fully experiencing them until later because of dissociation (Caruth, 1991). When our personal through lines are interrupted, instead of a conventional narrative, we are left with fragmented, psycho-physical experiences (Caruth, 1996).

By extension, queer constructions of identity may be experienced as the memory of emotionally powerful events that are not necessarily organized into a coherent story, as trauma and dominant cultural scripts stifle our ability to make sense of our lives, and as shame prevents us from working through inherent tensions and aporias. Sedgwick (2003) argues that queer identity might be conceptualized as one that turns most durably on shame, and Cvetkovich (2012) believes that depression is intimately connected with a failure to conform. Butler (1997, p. 144) suggests that this has much to do with gender identity: "rigid forms of gender and sexual identification, whether homosexual or heterosexual spawn forms of melancholy." In her book about happiness, Ahmed (2010, p. 37) takes this into the realm of physiology when she writes that

> when we feel pleasure from [socially acceptable] objects, we are aligned; we are facing the right way. We become alienated . . . when we do not experience pleasure from the proximity to objects that are already attributed to being good.

After reading this chapter several times, and strengthening it through several drafts with her suggestions and comments, Val sent me the following final comment, which I include in its entirety:

> I wrote that piece at Old Lesbian Writers and Scholars (OWLS) around 2008 or so, I think. I retired at the end of 2014. A year or so prior to my retirement, as a Member of the Kwantlen Faculty Association Executive, I finally persuaded them to have an LGBTQ Faculty Representative on the Executive (something I had tried unsuccessfully to achieve twice before). I stood for and got elected as the first LGBTQ rep Kwantlen had. That was coming out hugely. Perhaps some of that writing pushed that agenda more strongly for me. (Innes, personal communication, May 2020)

Although the ubiquitous "coming out" story is one that queer individuals depend upon as a bookmark in their life stories, even the act of coming out is complicated and recursive as it often spans several life events, and is, in a sense, never completed (even Val's work as an LGBTQ rep might be framed by some as a reversion to the queer norm). Several queer elders in my programs have written about the necessity of coming out toward the ends of their lives to a revolving door of home health care workers (some with cultural biases against LGBTQ clients).

No culture is absolute, however "natural" it might feel, and yet, as cultural systems, particularly public education, have focused on the reproduc-

tion of canonical knowledge, normative assumptions, and radical individu-
ation, those on the margins have been largely ignored. For the queer subject,
this has often led to feelings of dissatisfaction, disassociation, shame, and
depression. To be consciously queer, or to have critical queer consciousness,
is to understand that the queer body is a "situation," as de Beauvoir (1989)
has put it, rather than a given, and our through lines can seem more recursive than linear, as we come out later in life, experiment with relationships
(such as serial monogamy or polyamory), and invent our own rituals and
rites of passage. To know that our realities are constructed is to understand
that human subjects and realities, including queer ones, are inherently fictive—a situation that opens up possibilities for creative transgression.

References

Ahmed, S. (2010). *The promise of happiness*. Duke University Press.

Berlant, L. (2010). Cruel optimism. In M. Gregg & G. Seigworth (Eds.), *The affect theory reader* (pp. 93–118). Duke University Press.

Britzman, D. P. (2006). *Novel education: Psychoanalytic studies of learning and not learning* (Vol. 300). Peter Lang.

Brown, R. M. (1977). *Rubyfruit jungle*. Bantam Books.

Butler, J. (1997). *The psychic life of power*. Stanford University Press.

Caruth, C. (1991). Introduction. *American Imago, 48*(4), 417–424.

Caruth, C. (1996). *Unclaimed experience: Trauma, narrative, and history*. Johns Hopkins University.

Cvetkovich, A. (1995). Sexual trauma/queer memory: Incest, lesbianism and therapeutic culture. *GLQ: A Journal of Lesbian and Gay Studies, 2*(4), 351–377.

Cvetkovich, A. (2012). *Depression: A public feeling*. Duke University Press.

D'Augelli, A. & Grossman, A. (2001). Disclosure of sexual orientation, victimization, and mental health among lesbian, gay, and bisexual older adults. *Journal of Interpersonal Violence, 16*(10), 1008–1027. http://jiv.sagepub.com/content/16/10/1008

de Beauvoir, S. (1989). *The second sex*. Vintage.

Dimock, C. (2012, July 24). What's queer about psychoanalysis? In *Freud, gender studies, Lacan, Literature, mythology, polymorphous perversity*. The Qouch. Retrieved October 15, 2015, from http://theqouch.com/2012/07/24/whats-queer-about-psychoanalysis-2/#more-456

Felman, S., & Laub, D. (1992). *Testimony: Crises of witnessing in literature, psychoanalysis, and history*. Routledge.

Freud, S. (1919). The uncanny. In *Collected Papers* (Vol. 4, pp. 368–407). Hogarth Press.

Giddens, A. (1991). *Modernity and self-identity*. Stanford University Press.

Haas, A. P., Eliason, M., Mays, V., Mathy, R. M., Cochran, S. D., D'Augelli, A. R., & Litts, D. A. (2011). Suicide and suicide risk in lesbian, gay, bisexual, and transgender populations: Review and recommendations. *Journal of Homosexuality, 58*(1), 10–51.

Hall, R. (1981). *The well of loneliness*. Avon.

Luria, H., Seymour, D.M., Smoke, T. (2006). *Language and linguistics in context: Readings and applications for teachers.* Lawrence Erlbaum Associates.

Massumi, B. (2010). The future birth of the affective fact. In M. Gregg, G. Seigworth, S. Ahmed, & B. Massumi (Eds.). *The affect theory reader* (pp. 52–71). Duke University Press.

Moon, L. T. (2006). The Heterosexualisation of emotion. *The Psychologist, 19* (1), 22-23.

Phillips, A. (Ed.). (2006). *The Penguin Freud reader.* Penguin.

Pillemer, D. B., Desrochers, A. B., & Ebanks, C. M. (1998). Remembering the past in the present: Verb tense shifts in autobiographical memory narratives. In C. P. Thompson et al. (Eds.), *Autobiographical memory: Theoretical and applied perspectives* (pp. 145–162). Lawrence Erlbaum.

Robson, C., & Sumara, D. (2007–2009). *OWLS research transcripts of discussions* [Unpublished raw data]. University of British Columbia, Vancouver, BC.

Roediger III, H., Dudai, Y., & Fitzpatrick, S. (Eds.). (2007). *Science of memory: Concepts.* Oxford University Press.

Sedgwick, E. (2003). *Touching feeling: Affect, pedagogy, performativity.* Duke University Press.

Shields, C. (2002). *Unless.* Random House.

Sumara, D. (2008). Small differences matter: Interrupting certainty about identity in teacher education. *Journal of Gay and Lesbian Issues in Education, 4*(4), 39–58.

Sutton, J. (2010). Memory. In *The Stanford encyclopedia of philosophy.* Retrieved July 19, 2020 from *The Stanford encyclopedia of philosophy*

TED. (2009, October 7). *The danger of a single story | Chimamanda Ngozi Adichie* [Video]. YouTube. http://www.youtube.com/watch?v=D9Ihs241zeg

CHAPTER FIVE

Collectivity

A NUMBER OF THEORISTS who work with autobiographical methods (Butt et al., 1992; Butt & Raymond, 1989; Davies & Gannon, 2006; Haug, 1992) have argued that the kind of work I describe in this book is conducted most effectively in collective collaborations. In this chapter, I consider and support this claim and then offer some practical suggestions as to how such robust collectives might be constructed following feminist activist principles. My reflections are rooted in my work over the years with several arts collectives, but I have chosen what I believe to be the most useful exemplar: The Queer Imaging & Riting Kollective for Elders (Quirk-e).

Long (2003) has spoken to the ongoing interest of women in learning and reflection and their ability to create and maintain informal spaces of learning such as crafting circles and book clubs. The feminist scholar Frigga Haug (1992) builds on this robust history as she reports on her educational practices based on the feminist consciousness-raising groups of first-wave feminism. Haug (1992, p. 9) argues that the oppression of women is structural and systemic as it operates through the operations of family and wage labor. Pointing to the general lack of emotional and social support for those who wish to walk away from traditional roles, she argues that there are few opportunities for women to build confidence or to develop their skills. "If women are to improve their position," Haug (1992, p. 10) writes, "they need a collective, a culture of their own." She goes on to suggest that one goal of such a collective might be the collective writing of stories as a way to find out about life. She believed that such language schools can successfully combine grassroots activities with research or, as she put it, detective work or critical investigation.

More recently, Haug's collaborative critical creative agenda has been taken up in other feminist projects. For instance, Davies and Gannon (2006,

p. 10) and some of their academic colleagues wrote together to explore a common theme: girlhood. They wrote stories about the kind of memory I have called a flashbulb or episodic memory. "As a rule of thumb," they suggest, the memory "should take place in one or two minutes" (Davies & Gannon, 2006, p. 10). The stories are read aloud and the group listens carefully, particularly on the lookout for "explanations or clichés" and the "emotional and embodied detail of the story." They represent their findings in a seamlessly coauthored text. In another example, Lather and Smithies engaged a group of women living with HIV in autobiographical methods to investigate the ways in which their lives were impacted by AIDS. Their book *Troubling the Angels* (Lather & Smithies, 1997) was produced jointly by these women and the researchers. The stories of the women are given prominence, and the more theoretical writing of the researchers is relegated to the bottom of the page. In this way, the usual power dynamic, in which the researcher interprets and analyzes the data harvested from participants, is reversed.

Although it is true that women have a strong tradition of collaborative work, they are not the only ones to have done so. Many First Nation peoples have used talking circles for millennia and still do as they seek restorative justice in various social contexts (Dennis, 2010). I argue that it is possible to construct arts-based communities in all marginalized populations and that this is an important form of social and political activism. When bodies of artistic work are constructed, they serve to represent lived experiences so that they can be made visible and examinable. By using texts as commonplaces for shared interpretations and discussions, learners can examine their personal and cultural situations. By creating and performing them, they may be able to recover experiences lost to insidious trauma and thus come to understand their situations differently. As I have mentioned earlier, queer and feminist scholar Ann Cvetkovich (2003) has described this process as creating "an archive of feelings," as she argues that the emotions that we have repressed become a mode of resistance to cultural norms once they have been articulated. I return to this possibility in Chapter 11.

In 2007, I established a writing group for old and queer people of all genders, joining forces in this venture with the Generations Project, a program serving the needs of queer elders, located within QMUNITY, an organization that supports queer life and activities across British Columbia. The writing group became popular and quickly grew in size. When our modest funding came to an end, the members of the group were determined to continue the work and brokered further funding.

As we decided to focus on a queer activist agenda, my role shifted from that of the traditional writing teacher, evolving into what Gramsci (1971) has called an "organic intellectual," someone with access to education and theoretical understandings who is embedded in a learning collective and able to serve its social and intellectual goals. Rather than operating as a detached researcher or teacher with a separate agenda, the organic intellectual subscribes to the political agenda of the group and supports its activities by sharing his or her expertise and knowledge. Gramsci argued that education actually creates the political foundations of the state and that scholars are never disinterested but a product of their socioeconomic circumstances. The role of the traditional scholar is to perpetuate the status quo. The role of the critical scholar is to disturb and overthrow it. As Said (1994) has put it, the specific role of the public intellectual to "overcome habits of expression [that] that already exist, one of whose main functions is to preserve the status quo, and to make certain that things go smoothly, unchanged, and unchallenged."

Working with this group was an education that radically altered my approach to autobiographical work. As our mission became political as well as artistic, members of the group with considerable experience as social activists shared their knowledge and perspectives, and power was thus decentralized to some extent, although not entirely. As an artist, performer, and social activist, I had the skills, background, and artistic vision necessary to organize showcases for the work that was emerging and encouraged the group to spill out beyond the walls of the seniors' center, where we met on a weekly basis, to become a public presence. We began to offer readings not just for friends and family (although they began to attend) but also for other seniors, health care workers, people in recovery, university students, and members of the public. I also recruited a graphic artist and photographer, who taught the group skills in new media. For my part, I continued to set writing prompts and to offer critique. I also drew drawing on my theatre background as I introduced playwriting and polished performance skills.

Through a happy confluence of circumstances, the group was ultimately adopted by the Vancouver Parks Board as part of a larger research project, the Arts Health and Seniors Project. For 14 years, I served as writer-in-residence for the collective, which still meets on a weekly basis at a senior center on the east side of Vancouver, now as a peer-led group. Their public events over the last 14 years have included several theatrical shows, a display of digital imagery at our downtown public library, digital videos, a human library, and a display of the memory boxes referenced in Chapter 2. Their written productions have included an annual anthology of written and graphic memoir. The most recent, *Basically Queer* (Robson et al., 2017), was published by a global publisher, Peter Lang Books. This text was co-written with another collective composed of queer youth, Youth for a Change. Later in the book (see Chapter 12), I talk further about this and other projects the two groups completed, which serve as rare examples of intergenerational collaborations in the queer community.

As the collective gained momentum and built a strong reputation, we began to form alliances and partnerships with other organizations. Our anthology, *The Bridge Generation* (Robson & Blair, 2014) was written to represent the experiences of older queers through the decades. Its six sections offer writings and graphic art covering the 1940s and 1950s through to the 2010s. Each section was organized and edited by an editorial team of Quirk-e members, who set writing prompts and reviewed the work submitted to their section of the text. The Vancouver Public Library dedicated a librarian to helping us research these periods, through books and microfiche periodicals. Dr. Elise Chenier, a queer historian and founder of the Archives of Lesbian Testimony, met with the group to offer feedback on their work, suggest other research sources, and offer her own insights into the queer histories of the periods we were writing about. She provided historical overviews to each of the book's sections.

Traditional arts workshops follow the studio model, in which artists work side by side on a common task and skills are introduced first and worked on in exercises that isolate and focus on those skills and do not necessarily strive for general or universal significance. Rather, their completion is seen as "practice" as learners embark on a journey toward "crafty" expression. The teacher is seen as an expert who offers advice, mediates discussions, and acts as the final arbiter of excellence. Students are positioned as learners and amateurs, and their work is seen as separate from its cultural context. The model that evolved in Quirk-e is entirely different in that learners work together on meaningful projects designed to generate cultural and social change. The teacher is still seen as an expert and facilitator but one who is decentered in the creative process and able to step aside to allow others to emerge as confident leaders and truth tellers. The work of the collective is seen as meaningful, socially engaged, and capable of challenging common assumptions and normative discourses.

This kind of work spills over the temporal and geographical boundaries of weekly meetings as it takes on some of the social, physical, and emotional issues that older queers engage with on a quotidian basis. The members of the Quirk-e collective are proud that their work serves to increase public awareness of the concerns and experiences of older queers and feel a strong sense of connection with the group. They socialize with each other, meeting to hike, write, go out to events, and help each other out with practical tasks like moving house. Research attached to the project from the University of British Columbia found that arts engagement had a profound positive impact on members in terms of their physical, emotional, cognitive, mental, and social health (Phinney et al, 2014). This outcome is particularly important for queer elders, who are less likely to be married, less likely to have children or to find their children supportive if they do have them (Fredricksen-Goldsen et al., 2013). They are also more likely to live alone and to feel lonely. The health impacts of exposure to discrimination are far-reaching and include increased risk of mental illness (Brotman et al., 2001; Cabaj & Stein, 1996). LGBT people are more likely to be depressed, to be disabled (Fredriksen-Goldsen et al., 2013), to have experienced various forms of trauma, and to have abused drugs and alcohol (Choi & Meyer, 2016). They are also at greater financial risk, because of discriminatory access to legal and social programs and lifetime disparity in earnings (Choi & Meyer, 2016). In the absence of traditional family and social networks, the construction of queer communities of support becomes much more important.

Collectives do not automatically occur just because you seat a number of people around a table and ask them to discuss a topic and "report back." In the remainder of this chapter, I consider some of the challenges and pedagogical demands of this kind of work.

Quirk-e illustrates the power of collaborative arts collectives to generate social change and address marginalization and common cultural assumptions. However, the process of co-constructing a sustainable and democratic collective is not without its challenges. Davies and Gannon (2006) note a range of problems in their chapter on the struggles of collaborative writing, mainly frustration with their own creative processes, the trauma generated by difficult memories, and the unequal power dynamics that existed in their collective.

In my experience, many students find the same problems, particularly those regarding power dynamics. In an undergraduate course I taught recently (on Queer Collective Arts Activism at Simon Fraser University), I asked the students to freewrite about their experiences with group work. The majority said that they detested it, at least as it is commonly organized by their professors. They said that a few students commonly do all the work, but the lazy students still get the same grade. The term *group work*, they suggested, is often a misnomer because one or two students take over the direction of the group just to get a plan that they can share with their teacher. Finally, it seemed to them that group work is often "busywork" set by teachers to avoid teaching from the front of the class.

As Quirk-e evolved, I found it vital to reconstruct our pedagogies and, specifically, to encourage the members of the group to be more conscious of the requirements of group processes. We archived and institutionalized all the conclusions we came to so that we were able to refer to the agreements we reached through our discussions of what made our decisions and conversations seem equitable and accessible. The handouts and documents we produced were of particular value to new members, but it is also true to say that they served as reminders to all of us. In the following, I touch briefly on the areas we covered.

I will begin with the problem of overtalking. "Even in consciousness-raising groups," Haug (1992, p. 19) lamented, "everyone sits waiting for her turn and would far rather talk than listen." This was a real problem in the collective's early days, particularly so because the collective was large and coeducational. There were rarely fewer than 20 members who showed up, some of them male and thus more used to talking more frequently and at greater length than their female counterparts. (This did not go down well in with the lesbian activists in the group!) We soon found that a "quick" check-in around the room could easily take an hour, and this represented half our weekly workshop time together. Although small-group work offered greater opportunities to discuss matters more equitably, certain discussions were more effectively conducted in the whole group. These included making key decisions, listening to people's opinions on important topics, and hearing what was going on in people's lives, particularly after a break for the holidays (notoriously difficult times for many queer individuals).

I decided to experiment with "speed talking," as I pointed out the dilemma (we wanted to hear from everyone but didn't want to spend a whole session on it). We began by giving each member 2 minutes to share their thoughts and appointed a timer who would give a warning at 90 seconds and cut the speaker off at 2 minutes. There was a little resistance as people often felt that their insights and comments deserved extra time, but after a while, the group became quite skilled at offering targeted and considered comments quickly.

As they saw that everyone had their turn, and the group moved forward efficiently, the Quirk-es became more adept at managing conversations this way. The timer became less necessary as people became used to being succinct. We were able to move to 1-minute check-ins, and even "quick hits" of a few seconds, as we needed to take a quick poll or temperature test. One of the benefits of this way of working is that it precludes the dominance of the conversation by more vocal or persuasive members, particularly those who are perceived to have more status within the group. The image we used for our check-ins was often that of the poker game in which everyone "lays their cards on the table." Rather than one or two people setting the tone for the conversation, everyone gets to have a say, and this makes it easier for those who have dissenting voices.

We also discussed the ways we conducted conversations and made decisions in smaller breakout groups, as problems with overtalkers and dominant individuals began to emerge. We co-created several sets of guidelines for small-group process and composition. First, we decided that the clique is an enemy of democratic dialogue, and so rather than having people choose who to work with (based on social preference), we formed groups along the lines of interest in the topic (as in the editorial teams for *The Bridge Generation*; Robson & Blair, 2014) or the genre of the work (for instance, graphic, poetic, theatrical, or prose). For more general discussions, I assigned groups randomly (usually by counting off). This meant that everyone had the expectation of getting to know and work with many different people in the course of a year. As a side note, I did get several requests for special treatment in this regard, as people talked to me privately to tell me that they simply "could not work in a group with X or Y." I rejected all such requests, although I did offer to broker conversations and mediations between conflicting parties. It seemed to me that being able to work together, despite personality conflicts, is a cornerstone of democratic dialogue and a necessary basis for group cohesion—its own version of Oliver's (2001) "working through."

One of the key pedagogical skills for the facilitator in this kind of work is knowing what method to use when. As the group became popular and oversubscribed, I began to work with co-lead or assistant artists, many of them young, and most of them with very little background in collective work. Their biggest challenge was to know what decisions the entire group should discuss and process together, what could be done in small groups, what decisions we could make as facilitators without discussion, and what decisions were a matter of individual preference. These are important pedagogical choices—a matter of classroom management, as it were—but they are also political and artistic.

In an arts collective, one must always protect the integrity of the individual artist. Although art can be made in a collective, it is not usually made collectively. The overall direction and artistic goals of a project must be discussed so that everyone buys into the current project. However, the individual artist must always have final say in the production of their own work. They are the only ones who can make the artistic decisions necessary to complete it to their satisfaction; although they will obviously take critique into account, they have no obligation to accept suggestions. Practical concerns, on the other hand, are the job of the facilitator, who does not need to bother the artists with them. An important part of the facilitator's role is to have the process run smoothly and almost invisibly around minor concerns while being transparent and dialogic about decisions that matter.

Most readers of this book will likely be aware of the constant need to negotiate the difference between consensus and majority decisions and when each is appropriate. Again, this depends entirely on the type of decision being made. Less important decisions can be made by a quick discussion followed by a vote. Weightier decisions, particularly with regard to emergent artistic directions, may need consensus. A consensus occurs when all members of the group feel that they are able to live with the decision made. Once consensus is reached, all members are required to buy into that decision without overdue complaints. Although further discussion might occur and the consensus might be reexamined, it is necessary for the group's health and ability to act that all parties are on board and committed. I found that making this distinction clear and understood was perhaps the most important in terms of group cohesion.

In all these discussions, members of a collective need to understand how to deal with conflict responsibly. Even older adults who are used to working in democratic organizations, like the members of Quirk-e, are prone to complain to the teacher about decisions they disagree with or, indeed, about the ways that they have been treated by others. This kind of triangulation, in which one person draws another person, usually one perceived to have authority, must be actively discouraged in the collective.

On only a few occasions I have found that irreconcilable differences bring communications to an impasse. On these occasions, we have had great success by working through a process of discernment. Borrowed from processes used by many contemporary church ministries (Austin, 2019), the form of discernment I use is a talking circle in which everyone speaks to the contention under investigation without interruption and as far as possible, without debating or questioning each other. A tight focus is maintained on how people feel about the issue rather on the construction of arguments for or against a particular decision. There is no interruption, cross talk, or time limit set for each person's sharing, and people may speak in any order but only once. It is a method that has proved effective in freeing up emotional logjams and generating mutual understandings and acceptance.

The following text (table 5.1) is from a handout that was co-created by Quirk-e and then given to all members when they joined. As you will see, it defines the mission of the group, so that new members understand its goals and its methods of working together, and it offers some simple, clear advice on respectful communications:

Groups need to pay close attention to process as well as product. They need to encourage quiet members to speak and to listen carefully and actively. They need to have mechanisms in place to ensure equal attention and airtime. They need to consider respectful but forthright communication. They need to record the decisions they have made so that they are not constantly reinventing their structures, although these structures might still evolve. In my work with

Table 5.1: *Introduction to Quirk-e*

Introduction to Quirk-e
The Queer Imaging & Riting Kollective for Elders was formed in 2006. The group has expanded to 27 members and performs regularly in public venues. The forms of art offered are generally writing and imagery, which are conducted under the direction of the two artists, Kelsey Blair and Claire Robson. Though there's a high degree of input from the group and much collaborative work, the group is not a collective in that all decisions are not made by consensus. For example, the lead artists decide on artistic direction for each year, offer critique on works in progress, and make most of the editorial decisions about what will be included in anthologies and shows. The group defines its mission as follows: Quirk-e works to change the world with its stories, while providing a safe place to nurture a vibrant entertaining voice for the senior queer citizens of Vancouver. We have experienced discrimination in our youth and some of us may be facing old age single, disabled and isolated. But we are nonetheless a "discordant and unruly choir, insisting, despite the odds, on showing the height, depth and breadth of our experiences." Because they see the group as a vehicle for activism and advocacy, members commit to showing up regularly and on time and also to contributing wholeheartedly to the project. Quirk-e is not just a "drop in social" group—though we do support each other and have fun, we work very hard. While we try to make the process as safe as possible, Quirk-e is engaged in making powerful, polished art. This can be challenging and even uncomfortable at times.
Some Dos and Don'ts for Quirk-e Communication
DO
• Wait to be acknowledged before speaking
• Speak one at a time
• Speak only for yourself
• Try to be positive
• Contribute to the collective
DON'T
• Interrupt
• Speak over other people
• Speak for others
IF YOU HAVE A COMPLAINT
• Think carefully about what bugs you and what you'd like to change. It's easier for the other person to hear you if what you say is clear and specific.
• Raise concerns with the person or people who you want to make that change, rather than someone you feel might be 'on your side.' Avoid splitting and triangulation.
• If you really can't do that, you can raise complaints with Claire or Kelsey. However, we'll need your permission to share the conversation/complaint if we are to do anything.

many collectives, I have found that having the group consider them first builds trust in the group process that is vital to sharing difficult and emotional work.

Oliver (2001) has called for forms of witnessing that are dialogic and democratic, rather than antagonistic and oppositional. The pedagogical suggestions that I have offered in this chapter draw from this important philosophical distinction. Building this culture of true collectivity takes time, but it is worth it because it enables us to "recognize ourselves as subjects or active agents through recognition from others" (Oliver, 2001, p. 4). It is particularly important for those of us who identify as queer to rewrite heteronormative discourses by writing our own frank accounts that help us to represent, understand, and normalize our experiences. As we construct new life narratives and coherent through lines, we necessarily question and complicate the narratives we have been told or the narratives we have constructed. It can be a difficult and confusing project. The support of an honest, functional, effective, and democratic community of practice can help us navigate this kind of ambiguity. In the next chapter, I consider some other means of navigating difficult and uncertain memories.

References

Austin, N. (2019, October 16). *Discernment as a work of the church*. Thinking Faith. https://www.thinkingfaith.org/articles/discernment-work-church

Brotman, S., Ryan, C., & Cormier, R. (2003). The health and social service needs of gay and lesbian elders and their families in Canada. *The Gerontologist, 43*(2), 192–202. doi:10.1093/geront/43.2.192

Butt, R., & Raymond, D. (1989). Studying the nature and development of teachers' knowledge using collaborative autobiography. *International Journal of Educational Research, 13*(4), 341–466.

Butt, R., Raymond, D., McCue, G., & Yamagishi, L. (1992). Collaborative autobiography and the teacher's voice. In I. Goodson (Ed.), *Studying teachers' lives* (pp. 51–98). Taylor & Francis.

Cabaj, R. P., & Stein, T. S. (1996). *Textbook of homosexuality and mental health*. American Psychiatric Press.

Choi, S. K., & Meyer, I. H. (2016). *LGBT aging: A review of research findings, needs, and policy implications*. The Williams Institute.

Cvetkovich, A. (2003). *An archive of feelings: Trauma, sexuality, and lesbian public cultures*. Duke University Press.

Davies, B., & Gannon, S. (Eds.). (2006). *Doing collective biography*. Open University Press.

Dennis, L. (2010). *Talking Circles: An Indigenous-centered method of determining public policy, programming and practice*. The School of Public Administration, The University of Victoria, BC. https://dspace.library.uvic.ca:8443/bitstream/handle/1828/8304/Dennis_Loretta_MPA_2010.pdf?sequence=1&isAllowed=y

Frederiksen-Goldsen, K. I., Kim, H-J., Barkan, S. E., Muraco, A., & Hoy-Ellis, C. P. (2013). Health disparities among lesbian, gay, and bisexual older adults: Results from a population-based study. *American Journal of Public Health, 103*(10), 1802–1809.

Gramsci, A. (1971). The intellectuals. In Q. Hoare & G. Nowell Smith (Trans. & Eds.), *Selections from the prison notebooks* (pp. 3–23). International Publishers.

Haug, F. (1992). *Beyond female masochism: Memory work and politics.* Verso.

Lather, P., & Smithies, C. (1997). *Troubling the angels: Women living with HIV Aids.* Westview/Harper Collins.

Long, E. (2003). *Book clubs: Women and the uses of reading in everyday life.* University of Chicago Press.

Oliver, K. (2001). *Witnessing: beyond recognition.* University of Minnesota Press.

Phinney, A., Moody, E. M., & Small, J. A. (2014). The effect of a community-engaged arts program on older adults' wellbeing. *Canadian Journal on Aging, 33*(3), 336–345.

Robson, C., & Blair, K. (Eds.) (2014). *The bridge generation.* Lulu.

Robson, C., Blair, K., & Marchbank, J. (Eds.). (2017). *Basically queer: An intergenerational introduction to LGBTQA2S+ lives.* Peter Lang.

Said, E. (1994). *Representations of the intellectual.* Vintage Books.

CHAPTER SIX

Writing About Painful Topics

I am the arrow shaft, carved along my length by unexpected lights and gashes from the very sky, and this book is the straying trail of blood.
—Annie Dillard (1990, pp. 19–20)

A T THE BEGINNING OF the workshops I teach, people often ask me if I intend to discuss issues of "safety." Instead, I usually remind them that making art is inherently dangerous, and although I offer strategies for dealing with the strong feelings that may emerge in the creative process, I cannot guarantee to protect them from psychic pain. Indeed, the writing prompts I (and most other writing teachers) set are often specifically designed to invite what Dillard (1990) describes as the "shedding of blood." The most popular guide for beginning writers is Natalie Goldberg's (1986) classic *Writing Down the Bones*, which has sold more than a million copies and has been translated into 12 languages. Here is one example from her introductory list of prompts: "Write about leaving. Approach it any way you want. Write about your divorce, leaving the house this morning or a friend dying" (Goldberg, 1986, p. 21).

Writing teachers encourage difficult feelings because this is where passion and feelings reside.

Many years ago, a student of mine wrote an innocuous piece titled "A Day at the Lake." It was typical of her work, which often referenced imminent lurking danger that was miraculously avoided. In this particular instance, she wrote about walking by a frozen lake. She ventured out onto the ice, but although it creaked alarmingly, it did not break. Other people walked out on the ice, and once again, she was fearful, but nothing happened. As I have already suggested, the highly emotional material that we suppress sends hints and feelers out toward the conscious mind (Freud, in Phillips, 2006), in this sense, forgetting can be a kind of remembering. This writer's work offered a prime example. Struck by the imagery she had represented, I set her another exercise to complete: *Write about what would happen if the ice broke.* The next morning, I asked the student if she had had any luck completing the assignment. It had kept her up all night, she said. I invited her to share the piece, and the first sentence, read through tears, has remained with me: "I never touched the baby." What this writer had recalled was an incident from her early teens when she had sexually molested two of three children she was babysitting.

Disclosure of upsetting things is not the sole purpose of making art, but it is always a strong possibility. As I have worked with teachers in the public school system in the United States, the United Kingdom, and Canada, many of them have told me that one of the chief reasons they avoid teaching creative writing in their classrooms is that they worry that students may disclose difficult information. They are sharply aware of their legal obligation to report family problems, such as abuse or suicidal ideation, and they feel ill prepared to deal with difficult affective material. This raises interesting questions about how we train our teachers to deal with emotional issues, about our increasingly risk-averse culture, and about our failure to deal adequately with the emotional struggles that many of our students endure in silence. This is certainly true of many queer students, who still miss school because of homophobic bullying, have lower grades, are less likely to go to college, and more likely to suffer from depression and low self-esteem (Rodriguez-Hidalgo & Hurtado-Mellado, 2019).

As Langer (1957, p. 22) has pointed out, the inward life of human beings is grossly oversimplified in science and in our everyday use of language. She points out that "only the most striking [feelings] have names, like 'anger,' 'hate,' 'love,' fear,' and are collectively called 'emotion'" (Langer, 1957, p. 22) As Davis et al. (2008, p. 3) point out elsewhere, most analytic strategies actively seek to "draw a veil of silence around emotions and bodies." Works of art are our only opportunity to research these affective inner lives because they express our inward reality. It would seem to follow that pedagogies that open spaces for art making should take into account the feelings that might emerge in the pursuit. Yet this is a topic largely ignored both in the academy and in the popular literature on creativity, which privileges *craft*—with its associations of logic and practical skills—on one hand, and some kind of almost magical *creative process*—a black box that cannot be opened or examined—on the other.

This dichotomy that has plagued the entire project of education as it has fueled many debates in educational circles between whole language and phonics, back to basics versus the humanities, and, as Grumet (1981) has pointed out, the battle between the patriarchal project for the curriculum and the feminine one. However, because arts education necessarily involves entry into the world of affect, it is a debate that is of particular interest in our field. It is one thing to testify to the turtle swimming toward us from the depths of the lake. It is quite another to take the next step, what Oliver (2001) calls witnessing the event by recognizing and representing its significance. In this chapter, I suggest some ways that writers can usefully work with difficult or painful topics.

Therapy Versus Art

First, it is important to draw a theoretical and practical distinction between doing art and doing psychoanalysis or therapy, although for sure, the two are connected. Felman and Laub (1992) suggest that they are folded within each other, or *implicated*, as psychoanalysis points to the unconscious of literature, while literature is the unconscious of psychoanalysis. The teachers I worked with often commented on the fact that they are "not trained therapists" and thus do not have the skills necessary to deal with the strong feelings that might emerge in their students' creative work. Although it is true that many teachers don't have this kind of specialized training, it should not preclude engaging our students in art. Making art can be therapeutic, but it is not therapy, and conflating the two ways of processing experiences has served to limit the ways in which we construct our pedagogies.

Teachers can resolve their quandary by keeping therapeutic and creative goals separate. Rather than attempting to solve or engage with emotional issues that arise in their students' work, they can more usefully keep the focus on the work itself. When difficult material emerges in a student's writing, I stick to the job I know and understand, which is always to make the work stronger. Instead of turning attention to the students' feelings, I return it to the ways in which the work might be moved forward. I actively discourage displays of sympathy from others (other than passing the Kleenex). I may comment on the courage of the writer. I may check in with them at the end of the session and see if they might want to talk with other (trained) adults or, in the case of children, their parents or school counselors. I may acknowledge that the work is brave and difficult. Mainly, however, I will always return attention to the task in hand: What do we think about the structure? What else might the writer include? Where does the energy of the piece begin to ramp up? This clarity keeps everyone safe, and I believe that it is also respectful and what Oliver (2001) would call "response-able." The trauma occurred. The artist has born witness to it. The job of their audience is to respond to the witnessing, not the trauma itself. It takes courage to *recognize and represent*, and the fact that the artist has begun this work is what we can usefully honor and help forward to closer expression.

Pedagogical Considerations

There are pedagogical strategies that can help, and these all strive for the same goal: psychic detachment and thus protection from the difficult affective work of recognition. They amount to a kind of sleight of hand or distraction, as they encourage the writer to dissociate from the material, almost as if it happened to someone else.

Freewriting

Freewriting has a long tradition in the arts. Coleridge claimed to have composed *Kubla Khan* (1816) in one draft and without reflection. The notion was also taken up by surrealists such as Andre Breton (1934, para. 40), who explained automatic writing as "the dictation of thought, in the absence of all control by reason, excluding any aesthetic or moral preoccupation." Freud himself was a proponent of free association, encouraging his analysands to let go of conscious reflection in order to stumble upon insights. Freewriting is exactly that—a time to let go of the need to edit or judge what one is saying, to let the work surprise you.

The pedagogical structure I use for free writing exercises is pretty simple: I set a tight time limit, remind people to keep the pen moving (even if it is only to write nonsense), and discourage rereading, editing, crossing out, or taking the pen from the paper to think (this is the work of revision, which is the topic I cover in Part III). We cannot revise until we have unpacked our feelings, and in this early stage of the process, the inner critic and the editorial voice must be silenced, or we will tend to close down the process of recognition. Often, I will offer occasional reminders, such as "Keep the pen moving" or "Don't worry about sounding writerly." More often than not, this kind of mind dumping throws up at least one or two gems in the form of fresh insight, a memory one had forgotten, or a productive image.

Point of View

It can be useful to change the point of view if the work becomes difficult, for instance, by switching from the first person to the third person for the writer to achieve emotional distance from the content as it happens to "someone else." Autobiographical work can become claustrophobic, and jumping into someone else's head entirely can also offer refreshing new insight. One participant could find nothing positive to say about her mother until we encouraged her to write from her mother's point of view and she recalled how devastated her mother was by the death of her best friend, and she began to understand her mother's isolation and her disappointment that her only girl child was so unlike her. Zunshine (2006) has argued that reading fiction is a way to increase empathic understanding and that, by extension, adopting the persona of others in our life stories can increase and complicate our understandings of ourselves.

Form

Form imposes order on our chaotic inner worlds. As the poet Ann Sexton (cited in Salvio, 2007) put it, it is a cage that is capable of containing the wild animals we choose to put there. In Chapter 2, I included a quote from Judy Fletcher, who said that the physical challenges of making the box distracted her from its difficult content as she focused on the specific tasks involved rather than her feelings. The same can be said to be true of all the formal demands made by various genres and media, such as the plasticity of one's paint or the demanding shape and rhyme scheme of a sonnet. Paula Salvio (2006, p. 24) reminds us that for the poet Anne Sexton, writing was a way of reenacting private terror to "make a logic out of suffering." Although it is true that Sexton's life did not end well, Salvio posits that Sexton's art allowed Sexton to "make a new reality and become whole" at least temporarily (p. 24).

I have said that teaching skills and techniques in isolation can inhibit free expression. However, that does not mean that they should never be taught, only that they should not be taught in a vacuum. Once first drafts have been completed, it is useful to draw attention to the form that the work seems to wish to take or to offer formal structures as a means of exploring the work further. The following is one example, a piece of work by Gwyneth Bowen. It began with a casual conversation over coffee and snacks before one of my writing workshops. Douglas, who had been a minister before he came out as a gay man, was telling the few of us who had arrived early how much he missed the liturgy of the church and, particularly, the sensuous poetry of some of the psalms. As the rest of the group arrived, we had begun googling some of the psalms he remembered, and I invited Douglas to read The Song of Solomon for us in his full and glorious "ministerial" voice:

Song of Solomon 1 (King James Version)

1   The song of songs, which is Solomon's.

2   Let him kiss me with the kisses of his mouth: for. thy love is better than wine.

3   Because of the savour of thy good ointments thy name is as ointment poured forth, therefore do the virgins love thee.

4   Draw me, we will run after thee: the king hath brought me into his chambers: we will be glad and rejoice in thee, we will remember thy love more than wine: the upright love thee.

5   I am black, but comely, O ye daughters of Jerusalem, as the tents of Kedar, as the curtains of Solomon.

6   Look not upon me, because I am black, because the sun hath looked upon me: my mother's children were angry with me; they made me the keeper of the vineyards; but mine own vineyard have I not kept.

7 Tell me, O thou whom my soul loveth, where thou feedest, where thou makest thy flock to rest at noon: for why should I be as one that turneth aside by the flocks of thy companions?

8 If thou know not, O thou fairest among women, go thy way forth by the footsteps of the flock, and feed thy kids beside the shepherds' tents.

9 I have compared thee, O my love, to a company of horses in Pharaoh's chariots.

10 Thy cheeks are comely with rows of jewels, thy neck with chains of gold.

11 We will make thee borders of gold with studs of silver.

12 While the king sitteth at his table, my spikenard sendeth forth the smell thereof.

13 A bundle of myrrh is my well-beloved unto me; he shall lie all night betwixt my breasts.

14 My beloved is unto me as a cluster of camphire in the vineyards of Engedi.

15 Behold, thou art fair, my love; behold, thou art fair; thou hast doves' eyes.

16 Behold, thou art fair, my beloved, yea, pleasant: also our bed is green.

17 The beams of our house are cedar, and our rafters of fir.

We chatted for a while about some of the questions Douglas's reading raised for us. How come such explicitly sexual material was included in the Bible? What did it mean for us, as queer people, that the Bible, which typically frowns on sexual love except for the purposes of procreation, includes such an explicit account of heterosexual passion? It seemed to some of us to invalidate the objection made by religious people—that homosexuality was wrong because it failed to result in procreation, the sole purpose of intercourse. What did it mean for those of us who identify as Christian, or spiritual, that we have either been rejected by the church or chosen to remove ourselves from it? How far might we allow ourselves, or be allowed, access to the rituals, beliefs, and writings that helped form our youthful identities? What had our exclusion from the church stolen from us? How might we celebrate our own lives?

Seizing the pedagogical moment, I suggested that we reclaim the genre of the psalm. We worked together to identify some of its stylistic generic components—its rich, heady imagery, its lyric qualities, its urge to be read aloud, its passionate longing to spill over the boundaries of strict sense. Then using these stylistic formulae, we wrote our own "queer psalms." The following is one example, written by Gwyneth Bowen (a mother and grandmother) for all the young ones.

Psalm 69 (and All the Other Numbers)

O ye parents, ye elders, ye wise teachers, hear now my plea:
    for there is no time to be lost.
May the young ones revel in the Spring: it is their own true season.
Smile ye as they come nubile together; yay, bless them from afar as
    they frolic in the sun and in the moonlight.
For their smooth, strong limbs burn to run and play: their blood
    glows and verily merrily must obey the electric pull of flesh to
    flesh that then they may find bliss in sleep. long and untroubled.
The unloving ones, the desiccated, miserable, predatory or hide-
    bound ones shall be made to lay off, and shall be corralled
    away from the lustful young things that they may be insouci-
    ant and juicy may jubilously kiss whomever and wherever they
    wish and be curious as to the possibilities of protuberances and
    orifices.
Enquire not about the details of their playful or urgent exploring,
    for the stories will be theirs alone to whisper lickingly in each
    others' ears, or anon to fuel moaning solo action replays.
Yo, I thus entreat thee: for now is the time of the engorged peak of
    their desirous discoveries: and their memories, unsullied, will
    be their enduring pleasure; yay, even unto death.

Gwyneth's psalm serves as an illustration of several of the points I have made in this section of the book. It represents an act of reclaiming an iconic form, one regarded as "sacred." Gwyneth (personal communication, May 5th, 2020) had this to say about her composition:

> I liked the naughtiness of using psalm in a subversive way (although the Song of Songs got there first, not a psalm but included in the Bible and ignored by most people who actually read it) . . . as a therapist specializing in childhood sexual abuse I had/have huge anger at the fallout of sexual repression, so that was there too.

As one raised in the Christian Church, I still experience a certain frisson and an accompanying sense of liberation when Gwyneth reads her psalm in public. It serves her aim (and one of the broad aims of the collective): to creatively transgress our normative understandings and to question whatever is taboo and "institutional." Its inception also serves as an example of the queer pedagogies I have discussed in this section in that it emerged from a collective conversation rather than a teacher-led curriculum. Taking this a step further, as an organic intellectual, rather than a researcher or detached workshop leader, I paid careful attention to the affective and political discourse within the group and seized the pedagogical moment. In Chapter 4, I suggested that understanding that our realities are fictive opens up possibilities for creative transgression. Gwyneth's psalm serves as an excellent concluding example.

In this second part of the book, I have considered the processes of recognition and suggested that for those who identify as queer, these may be more complicated, recursive, and difficult, as the forces of resistance work through us and we re-collect and reorganize our narrative through lines from beyond the pale of normative discourse. I have also offered some collective pedagogical strategies for both embracing and navigating some of the difficult and productive feelings that might attend the curious artist on this autobiographical journey.

The next part is all about revision. When we know what the work wants, revision becomes a process of fully serving that intention, and the hard work of creation often happens after the first draft has been composed.

In Chapter 7, I discuss the permeable boundary between truth and fiction and the ethics of representation as I ask how much "the truth" exists or even matters. In Chapter 8, I offer some productive methods for revision, including imitation, changing point of view, and considerations of genre. In Chapter 9, I consider the challenges and rewards of peer critique and how it can be best facilitated.

References

Breton, A. (1934). *The manifesto of surrealism*. Tcg.us.edu/Classes/Jbutler/T340/SurManifesto/ManifestoOfSurrealism.htm

Davis, B., Sumara, D. & Luce-Kapler, R. (2008). *Engaging minds: Changing teaching in complex times*. Routledge.

Dillard, A. (1990). *Three by Annie Dillard: Pilgrim at Tinker Creek; An American childhood; The writing life*. Harper Perennial.

Felman, S., & Laub, D. (1992). *Testimony: Crises of witnessing in literature, psychoanalysis, and history*. Routledge.

Goldberg, N. (1986). *Writing down the bones*. Shambhala.

Grumet, M. (1981). Pedagogy for patriarchy: The feminization of teaching. *Interchange on Educational Policy, 12*(2–3), 165–184.

Langer, S. K. (1957). *Problems of art*. Scribner.

Oliver, K. (2001). *Witnessing: Beyond recognition*. University of Minnesota Press.

Phillips, A. (Ed.). (2006). *The Penguin Freud reader*. Penguin.

Rodriguez-Hidalgo, A.J. & Hurtado-Mellado, A. (2019). Prevalence and psychological predictors of homophobic victimization among adolescents. *International Journal of Environmental Research and Public Health, 16*(7), 1243.

Salvio, P. M. (2007). *Anne Sexton: Teacher of weird abundance*. State University of New York Press.

Zunshine, L. (2003). Theory of mind and experimental representations of fictional consciousness. *Narrative, 11*(3), 270–291. www.jstor.org/stable/20107319

PART III

REVISING

CHAPTER SEVEN

Truth

*Most of our mental and active life is of the immediate coping variety, which
is transparent, stable, and grounded in our personal histories. Because it is
so immediate, not only do we not see it, we do not see that we do not see it,
and this is why so few people have paid any attention to it until phenom-
enology and pragmatism, on the one hand, and new trends in cognitive
science, on the other hand, brought it to the fore.*

—Varela (1999, p. 19)

JAMES FREY'S 2003 MEMOIR, *A Million Little Pieces*, was picked as an
Oprah's Book Club selection and quickly became the number one paperback nonfiction book on Amazon. It was only when the myth-busting
website The Smoking Gun (2006) searched online for an author photograph
that they discovered that portions of Frey's story had been invented. Frey's
publisher, Random House (which had previously described the book in a
press release as "brutally honest," despite conducting no fact checks) admit-
ted on CNN News that on further investigation, it found that "a number
of facts had been altered and incidents embellished" (O'Brien & O'Brien,
2006, para. 76). They subsequently offered refunds to anyone who had
bought a copy. The Frey controversy could have been simply avoided by
publishing the book as a novel and is perhaps most compassionately seen as
a matter of inaccurate market placement rather than improper ethics, but
the incident raises some important questions about the relationship between
personal writing and personal truth.

This chapter takes a step back from the pedagogical practicalities I considered in the last part as it offers an overview of truth and fiction as it per-
tains to memoir and some reflections on the nature of vision and the very
possibility of "truth." If re-vision, as the etymology of the word implies,

is a process of "seeing again," then this seems a logical place to begin this section.

In terms of genre, memoir evolved from autobiography. This latter genre usually describes the entire span of someone's life (normally someone who is already of public interest, such as a famous artist or politician). Generally speaking, traditional autobiographies stick tightly to events as they occurred, although the author may well describe his or her responses and feelings about them. The memoir (sometimes called the "new" memoir to distinguish it from more traditional forms of autobiography) often focuses on a specific aspect or period of the narrator's life (say childhood) and is written with a theme or purpose in mind. *Homage to Catalonia* (Orwell, 1938) provides a useful example. Rather than detailing Orwell's entire life, it focuses on his experiences in the Spanish Civil War and is clearly written to decry the horrors of armed conflict.

New memoir employs the techniques of fiction to make the narrative vivid and generate emotional responses in the reader. Characters engage in dialogue, and detailed physical descriptions are offered. Frey defended the right of memoirists to draw on memories, as well as documented facts, and to create dramatic tension (Hagan, 2003). He had a point. If memoirists were to draw only on fact, their books would be much shorter and much less interesting. For instance, here is an extract from Frank McCourt's (1996) breakout memoir *Angela's Ashes*:

> It's dark on Atlantic Avenue and all the bars around the Long Island Railroad Station are bright and noisy. We go from bar to bar looking for Dad. Mam leaves us outside with the pram while she goes in or she sends me. There are crowds of noisy men and stale smells that remind me of Dad when he comes home with the smell of whiskey on him.
>
> The man behind the bar says, Yeah, sonny, whaddya want? You're not supposeta be in here, y'know.
>
> I'm looking for my father. Is my father here?" (p. 26)

Was every single bar on that specific night bright and noisy? Is the dialogue recorded exactly? The reader does not really care, accepting that the writer is re-creating the scene as he can best recall and adding details that may be factually inexact but serve to re-create a scene that actually occurred. Although we accept some degree of fictionalizing, what we would not accept is that McCourt did not have a father or that his father was not an alcoholic. When we read new memoir, we do so in the expectation that the techniques of literary invention serve to illustrate and represent events that actually happened. Where one stands in the controversy about Frey's (2003) work depends on where one draws the line on a highly permeable and ambiguous boundary between truth and fiction.

Perhaps a more productive question concerns our capacity to perceive the truth at all—indeed, the nature and even the existence of truth. This is the question I turn to next, as I begin with an example from Pulitzer Prize–winning novelist Annie Dillard. Here is an extract from *Pilgrim at Tinker Creek*:

> The artificial obvious is hard to see. My eyes account for less than one percent of the weight of my head; I'm bony and dense; I see what I expect. I once spent a full three minutes looking at a bullfrog that was so unexpectedly large I couldn't see it even though a dozen enthusiastic campers were shouting directions. Finally, I asked, "What color am I looking for?" and a fellow said, "Green." When at last I picked out the frog, I saw what painters are up against: the thing wasn't green at all, but the color of wet hickory bark." (Dillard, 1990, pp. 24–25)

Dillard draws a distinction here between the "natural" and the "artificial" obvious. The natural obvious is that which we expect to see, in this case, a smallish, generically green frog. The artificial obvious is that which the eye must be trained to see, or put another way, that which the more educated brain might expect—a large frog that is an unusual shade of dark green. Had Dillard been a naturalist who knew what bullfrogs looked like, she would have seen it more quickly. Had others not seen it before her, she might never have noticed it, and more important, she would never have known that she had not noticed it. What we already know influences our ability to see what is new.

Cognitive scientist and philosopher Francisco Varela (1992) makes the same point as Dillard in the quotation that opens this chapter. As he argues that most of our mental life is "of the immediate coping variety," Varela (1992, p. 19) suggests that we have to make sense of our perceptions of reality in order to even "get by" and that this business of getting by occupies most of our conscious life and the nature of our perceptions. As Dillard points out elsewhere (2009, p. 32–33), "for the newly sighted person, vision is pure sensation unencumbered by meaning." Those of us who have always been able to see have learned that distant objects look smaller than ones, or that there are such things as shadows. Importantly, these understandings and reinterpretations of the data received from our sense organs, understandings that allow us to cope and live our lives, have become unconscious and tacit, or "transparent," as Varela (1992) puts it. As Davis et al. (2008, p. 20) point out, "one of the tricks of consciousness" is that it "disguises the fact that it lags about a half-second behind actual events. That lag is needed for nonconscious processes to sort through, interpret, and select what will become conscious." Although we believe that our vision is a vision of a concrete universal reality that exists "out there," it is, in fact, a matter of interpretation, although as human beings, we have reached considerable consensus about what the world looks like.

This consensus is far from innocent, as our Eurocentric, normative agreements about what the world is like ignore other ways of knowing and perceiving. In his article "What Is It Like to Be a Bat?" Thomas Nagel (1974) convincingly argued that it is difficult, if not impossible, for human beings to close the gap between subjective and objective experiences of the world, especially when we are thinking about other life-forms. For instance, although we know that bats use sonar, we do not have that capacity and thus cannot even begin to extrapolate the inner life of the bat from our own experience. Given that we occupy such a small part of the planet (0.01% of its carbon weight), our view of reality is anthropocentric, and some have suggested that this blindness to the existences of nonhuman life-forms has contributed to our poor stewardship of the planet (Powers, 2019). Members of the disability community also seek to raise awareness of and respect for the ways in which they see and experience the world differently from the norm.

We humans are meaning-making creatures with a natural affinity for narrative construction (Carey, 2007). We stitch together gaps in our perceptions of reality to make sense of the world as our brains communicate with our sense organs far more than our sense organs communicate with our brains (Davis et al., 2008, p. 22). This situation is significant for educators, whose job it is to change and shape how the world is seen not by compelling others to see what we see but by "expanding the space of the possible" and open perception to new understandings (Davis et al., 2008, p. 20). It is difficult work precisely for the reasons Dillard and Varela have identified. When we do not see something because our sedimented histories, assumptions, and expectations make us unable to see it, we not only do not see it; we also do not know that we have not seen it. This will come as no surprise to the queer reader, for instance, the butch lesbian who is used to being read as male. Heteronormativity can limit learning before the act of conscious thought.

We construct our realities in the light of what we already know, and what we already know is communicated through various texts and technologies, including language, which Chomsky (cited in Jusczy, 2000, p. 21) suggests has become part of our genetic disposition, in that as humans have evolved, we have become "specially designed" to acquire complex grammars at even early stages of our development. "Language has become so integrated into human experience that it is not usually regarded as a human invention" (Sumara, 2008), but as something existing in its own right, like a mountain or a tree. In this process, our stories and grand narratives may become so invisible to us, so much a fact of life, that we perceive them as "just the way things are." Language both obstructs and impedes our perception.

If we look at the ways in which queer rights and queer culture have evolved, we can see the shifting complex relationship between language and queer identities. The contemporary use of "they" as a choice of pronoun for nonbinary or genderqueer people has aroused a great deal of protest, which is located largely, if not entirely, in societal norms. As Merriam-Webster (2020) has pointed out, there is no ground for objection on grammatical grounds because the pronoun *you* was originally plural and still takes a plural verb even when referring to a single person. *You are* is perfectly grammatical, and we have been using *they* to fill in for our lack of a gender-neutral pronoun for more than 600 years. The contestation is sociopolitical, and its eventual resolution will both reflect and change societal attitudes regarding how we perceive and talk about gender identifications.

This example serves to illustrate a key point: Changing language can change societal and individual attitudes. This is of particular importance for groups of people underrepresented in our joint interpretations of reality. Take, for instance, the language we have used to describe unwanted sexual advances by men. In the 1950s, we might have described it as "men just being men." In the 1970s, we began to describe it as "sexual harassment." Opening up our language has led, ultimately, to the #MeToo movement (Ohlheiser, 2017). This change in how we discuss and interpret male behaviors has led us to reexamine, or reperceive, behaviors such as the casting couch, once a Hollywood trope and now, with the conviction and sentencing of Harvey Weinstein, a crime. What once lay inside the pale now lies beyond it.

How does this relate to our considerations of truth in memoir?

Our contemporary popular fascination with our subjective inner lives is demonstrated by the pervasiveness of reality shows and news stories that focus on the sensational. Our interest in the lives of others seems inexhaustible in "the age of memoir." As Budd (2017) also pointed out in an article in the *Chicago Tribune*, many of these storytellers have been women. The backlash that this has generated often has misogynist undertones as some (largely male) critics have framed life writing as narcissistic, self-indulgent, and fluffy in comparison with more traditional or "serious" (read male) literary genres. One of many examples is offered in a recent article in the *New Yorker* (Tolentino, 2017): "These essays were mostly written by women. They came off as unseemly, the writer's judgment as flawed. They were *too* personal: the topics seemed insignificant, or else too important to be aired for an audience of strangers" (para. 1). It is certainly true that like other genres, memoir has suffered from a somewhat grisly interest in the dysfunction of others; the consequent repetition of certain popular tropes, such as the whacky but dysfunctional family; and narratives of redemption (such as Frey's).

It is also true, from a poststructural standpoint, that in some senses, the author is dead, as Barthes (1997) famously pointed out:

> Linguistically, the author is never more than the instance writing, just as I is nothing other than the instance saying I: language knows a "subject," not a "person," and this subject, empty outside of the very enunciation which defines it, suffices to make language "hold together," suffices, that is to say, to exhaust it.

> We know now that a text is not a line of words releasing a single "theological" meaning (the "message" of the Author-God) but a multi-dimensional space in which a variety of writings, none of them original, blend

and clash. The text is a tissue of quotations drawn from the innumerable centres of culture. (p. 115)

For sure, all texts are open to the interpretations of readers, and none of them are "original" in that they are unable to communicate outside or beyond the capabilities of language as we know it. Barthes's (1997) assertion, that the author draws entirely from the innumerable centres of culture s/he inhabits is inarguable. It is unwise to dismiss his concerns too quickly, as we consider the educational potential of working with life stories through artistic representations. Critics have pointed out the elitist and colonial assumptions inherent in "high art" (McDermott, 2010). In the academic world, and particularly in educational discourses, there has been a failure to theorize the work sufficiently or to develop robust methodologies (Robson & Sumara, 2016). In the writing world, and in my own research, there are plenty of narratives that serve to reinscribe epic narratives and normative accounts.

However, whether we believe them or not, the stories of our lives are told, despite these concerns, and it behooves us to join the party, especially if we belong to a marginalized population. Any form of speech, or even the very act of thinking, begins with private experience (Britzman, 2006, p. 66), and history itself is based on individual memories of what happened. Although these individual recollections have become codified and institutionally sanctioned, they are the narratives of victors, and these narratives serve to erase alternative accounts of our histories, particularly the histories of those who have been marginalized, ignored, or forgotten because they were traumatic (Felman & Laub, 1992). Firsthand accounts give back a central place to "the people who made and experienced history" as they complicate and trouble dominant narratives (Thompson, 2016, p. 3).

When language is understood in this way, as the site of competing discourses that give meaning to the world, it can become a place of exploration. Our lives are lived at that place where the private and the public meet, where abstract social systems such as class, family, religion, gender, and sexuality can actually be felt (Cvetkovich, 2003, p. 23). When we construct artistic archives of feeling, the impact of these abstract systems can become more conscious and more visible (Cvetkovich, 2003) as we "analyze and pry" (Dillard, 1990, p. 122). Jeanette Winterson (1995) put it this way:

When we tell a story, we exercise control, but in such a way as to leave a gap, an opening. It is a version, but never the final one. And perhaps we hope that the silences will be heard by someone else, and the story can continue, can be retold. (p. 8)

One of my research participants, Chris Spencer, put it this way:

It feels like I have changed a bit and changed my story. I had thought that my childhood was a long continuum of impositions that I had to tolerate. I now see my childhood in terms of a struggle, and the eventual emergence from an oppressive household.

In writing about her difficult relationship with her controlling mother, she was able to unearth stories of resistance and agency, such as walking down the street wearing a cowboy suit or earning her own money. As she wrote, at the insistence of the group, from her mother's point of view, she was able to enter, at least to a small extent, her mother's assumptive world and develop some empathy for her isolation and depression.

The sociologist Norman Denzin (1994, p. 295) has drawn our attention to what he has called a double crisis in contemporary academic discourse—the crisis of representation and the crisis of legitimization. He concludes that it is politically necessary to understand how power and ideology operate through systems of discourse as we ground our work in post-Marxist feminism. "A good text," he argues, "exposes how race, class, and gender work their ways in the concrete lives of interacting individuals" (Denzin, 1994, p. 298). Texts such as Joyce's *Ulysses*, he suggests, reproduce "multiple versions of the real" in a process that he calls "deconstructive verisimilitude" (Denzin, 1994, p. 300). The avant-garde postmodern writing sensibility introduced by Joyce suggests new writing formats such as narratives of the self, fiction, poetry, drama, performance science, polyvocal texts, responsive readings, aphorisms, comedy and satire, visual presentations, and mixed genres. He also points to Lather's (1986) notion of catalytic validity as a way to assess the impact of artistic research projects on its community in terms of empowerment and emancipation.

While I agree with Denzin's broad conclusions, I find it somewhat ironic and disappointing that he chooses a male writer to support them. After all,

Woolf was an exact contemporary of Joyce (they were born and died in the same years). Woolf's *The Voyage Out*, an equally polyvocal and impressionist novel, was published seven years before *Ulysses*. As they have often been denied access to other forms of media, women have always used writing and stories to interrogate their lived experiences, in the form of such texts as journals, poetry, recipe, and commonplace books. This work has presented vitally important alternative interpretations of historical events. Although much of it has been ignored and lost, there are a few notable exceptions, such as the following fragment by Sappho, written somewhere between 630 and 570 BCE. As she reframes the story of Helen, Sappho challenges patriarchal value systems of war and conquest to set against them the simple fact of subjective human desire: what one loves or desires.

> Some an army of horsemen, some an army on foot
> and some say a fleet of ships is the loveliest sight
> on this dark earth; but I say it is whatever you desire
> (Blundell, 1995, p. 89)

By way of conclusion, I suggest that all knowledge is partial, and all vision clouded by what we expect to see. Rather than focusing on the lost cause of absolute truth in depicting a reality that lies "out there," all we can do is represent our limited understandings and interpretations of what we see, particularly as we speak from positions on the margins or with voices that have been silenced or ignored. Those of us who have been regarded as other do so in the knowledge and hope that language itself can stretch and change to embrace the new meanings and understandings that we have to offer.

References

Barthes, R. (1977). *Image, music, text*. Hill and Wang.

Blundell, S. (1995). *Women in ancient Greece*. Harvard University Press.

Britzman, D. P. (2006). *Novel education: Psychoanalytic studies of learning and not learning* (Vol. 300). Peter Lang.

Budd, K. (2015). Does memoir belong to one gender? Chicago Tribune Retrieved July 19, 2020 from http://chicagotribune.com/entertainment/books/ct-prj-write-like-a-woman-ken-budd-20151112-story.html

Carey, B. (2007, May 22). This is your life (and how you tell it). *New York Times*. https://www.nytimes.com/2007/05/22/health/psychology/22narr.html

Cvetkovich, A. (2003). *An archive of feelings: Trauma, sexuality, and lesbian public cultures.* Duke University Press.

Davis, B., Sumara, D., & Luce-Kapler, R. (2008). *Engaging minds: Changing teaching in complex times.* Routledge.

Denzin, N. K. (1994). Evaluating qualitative research in the poststructural moment: The lessons James Joyce teaches us. *Qualitative Studies in Education, 7*(4), 295–308.

Dillard, A. (1990). *Three by Annie Dillard: Pilgrim at Tinker Creek; An American childhood; The writing life.* Harper Perennial.

Felman, S., & Laub, D. (1992). *Testimony: Crises of witnessing in literature, psychoanalysis, and history.* Routledge

Frey, J. (2003). *A million little pieces.* Doubleday.

Hagan, J. (March 3, 2003). Meet the staggering new genius. *Observer* https://observer.com/ 2003/02/meet-the -new-staggering-genius-2/

Jusczyk, P. (2000). *The discovery of spoken language*: MIT Press.

Lather, P. (1986). Issues of validity in openly ideological research: Between a rock and a soft place. *Interchange in Educational Policy, 17*(4), 63–84. doi:10.1007/BF01807017

McCourt, F. (1996). *Angela's ashes: a memoir.* Scribner.

McDermott, M. (2010). Outlaw arts-based educational research. *Journal of Curriculum and Pedagogy, 7*(1), 6–14. doi:10.1080/15505170.2010.10471306

Merriam-Webster (2010). Singular 'they.' Retrieved July 19, 2020 from merriam-webster.com/ words-at-play/singular-nonbinary-they

Nagel, T. (1974). What is it like to be a bat? *The Philosophical Review, 83*(4), 435–450.

O'Brien, S., & O'Brien, M. (2006, January 27). *A majority for Hamas could mean no peace in Middle East; Oprah faces off with author* [Television broadcast transcript]. CNN. http://transcripts.cnn.com/TRANSCRIPTS/0601/27/ltm.01.html

Ohlheiser, A. (2017, October 19). The woman behind 'Me Too.' *Washington Post.* https:// www.washingtonpost.com/news/the-intersect/wp/2017/10/19/the-woman-behind-me-too-knew-the-power-of-the-phrase-when-she-created-it-10-years-ago/

Orwell, G. (1938). *Homage to Catalonia.* Harvill Secker.

Powers, R. (2018). *The overstory.* Norton.

Robson, C., & Sumara, D. (2016). In memory of all the broken ones: catalytic validity through critical arts research for social change. *International Journal of Qualitative Studies in Education, 29*(5), 617–639. http://dx.doi.org/10.1080/09518398.2016.1139211

The Smoking Gun. (2006). *A million little lies.* http://www.thesmokinggun.com/documents/ celebrity/million-little-lies

Sumara, D. (2008). Small differences matter: Interrupting certainty about identity in teacher education. *Journal of Gay and Lesbian Issues in Education, 4*(4), 39–58.

Thompson, P. (2009) *The voice of the past: Oral history.* Oxford University Press.

Tolentino, J. (2017, May 18). The personal-essay boom is over. *The New Yorker.* https://www. newyorker.com/culture/jia-tolentino/the-personal-essay-boom-is-over

Varela, F. (1999). *Ethical know-how: Action, wisdom, and cognition.* Stanford University Press.

Winterson, J. (1995). *Art objects: Essays on ecstasy and effrontery.* Vintage Books.

CHAPTER EIGHT

Revision

I look into myself, and I see "there is no there there." I have no eye/I majestic and omniscient. I do, however, have hallucinations that present themselves to me with terrifying vigor. I do have storms and seizures of selfhood, brief and violent. For a moment I do see something, I understand, I am invigorated by the power of rationality and sense. But then I look up. I look up to see the things seen by that "she" who a moment ago was "I." Even as I describe that to myself, that self that was mine has dissolved and I am rummaging among the junk of what she has left behind . . . and that is all vision is: revisions coming at us at the speed of light. Writing presents to us the nullity of ourselves, the inaccuracies of our conceptions of selfhood. We are both nothing and everything—provisional, shifting, molten.

—Emanuel (1992, p. 256)

To our best knowledge, we have no eye/I, majestic and omnipotent, as the poet Lyn Emanuel (1992) has pointed out, only "storms and seizures of selfhood" that may indeed present themselves with great vigor—so much so that we actually believe in them. When we look up, we find that we see things differently because we are never the person we were before we looked up. Vision necessarily involves re-vision, as our eye and our consciousness adapt and adjust to fresh insights moment by moment, rendering our experiences of the world as "provisional, shifting, molten." There is no world "out there," only our constructions and deconstructions of it. Writing offers us the opportunity to understand that we are "nothing and everything." Revising our work can be difficult and confusing—one is often working with deep emotional material, and there is no right or wrong outcome. In this chapter, I both explore the challenges of revision and offer some pedagogical approaches I have found effective.

The importance of revision is fundamental to writing with insight, passion, and clarity. The poet Richard Tillinghast (2001, p. 245) has suggested that the ability to revise separates "the poet from the person who sees poetry as therapy or self-expression" and that it is the way to learn how to be "worth one's salt as a writer." There is a crucial difference between a promising first draft and a finished piece, and many putative writers stumble at this hurdle as their promising first drafts smolder, ignored in legions of journals and notebooks.

Much has been written to celebrate the success of phenomenological research methods, but much can also be learned by paying attention to our failures. Our research participants were no exception. The twin evils of resistance and avoidance dogged all the research projects discussed in this book. Our writers didn't make time for the work or they conveniently forgot it. Sometimes they turned up and talked about their ideas for the piece or, on one occasion, even attempted to offer a spontaneous on the spot improvisation of new iterations. When faced with the task of revising an emotionally demanding piece of writing, they prevaricated, avoided, delayed, and ultimately, several of them shelved it or moved on to easier work. "It was so hard to sit down and write this," said one. "I almost had to bully someone else into doing it" (Robson & Sumara, 2007, p.20). Of the six members of the Old Lesbian Writing Scholars (OWLS) writing group, perhaps only two or three pushed through the obstacles successfully to produce polished work. This is not to say that the work of the others was negligible or that they may have conducted their affective work in other ways or at other times.

Dillard (1990, p. 549) is one of the few writers commenting on this part of the writing process, as opposed to the production of first draft work. I therefore draw on her at some length in this chapter. In the following, she likens the process of revision to following a trail of breadcrumb into new territory:

> Is it a dead end, or have you located the real subject? You will know tomorrow, or this time next year. . . . The writing has changed, in your hands, and in a twinkling, from an expression of your notions to an epistemological tool. The new place interests you because it is not clear. You attend. In your humility, you lay down the words carefully, watching all the angles. Now the earlier writing looks soft and careless. Process is nothing; erase your tracks. The path is not the work. I hope your tracks have grown over; I

hope the birds ate the crumbs; I hope you will toss it all and not look back. (Dillard, 1990, p. 549)

If one has lost one's way on the trail, it is tempting to look for a guide who knows the area. Unfortunately (or fortunately), the trail is the vein of one's own sensibility, and ultimately, there are no yardsticks, rules, or even ways to measure one's progress in the journey. The fact that something has been published does not guarantee its worth, only that there is a market for that kind of writing. The fact that it has not been accepted for publication does not mean that it is unworthy of an audience. The work of the great Canadian writer and artist Emily Carr was ridiculed for much of her lifetime, simply because she had moved beyond local artistic conventions and was trying something new. To read Carr's (2005) autobiography is to marvel at her courage and conviction in the face of the contempt shown by local critics and her family. Writing groups are helpful but do not ultimately have any authority. Some members of one's writing group may love the ending of your piece, and an equal number may want you to change it. Giving up control to a well-established and knowledgeable writing coach will mean that you will write well but probably rather like him or her. Essentially, you are on your own in unchartered territory. Your life story is unique, and only you know how to tell it.

Although the distinction between editing and revision is permeable, it is nonetheless important that it is clearly drawn at the beginning of this discussion. When we edit our work, we are doing the housework rather than redesigning or remodeling our home. Editing involves correcting spellings, grammar, awkward phrasings, wordiness, and unnecessary complications and confusions. Often, these are a matter of correct, or at least current, grammatical and literary usage. The writer will find that editing does not affect the meaning or intention of the work but simply makes it more transparent so that the reader is not distracted by unfamiliar or eccentric use of words.

When we revise our work, we have two aims.

The first goal of revision is to ensure that we have told our current truth as we can best perceive it. As we have seen, this truth is often fleeting, partial, situated, and imagined. Unlike the scientist, who strives for universal insights in experiments that are repeatable, controlled, and lead to transferrable knowledge, the artist may choose to illustrate states of being that are temporary and unusual and exist as part of a shifting reality. For instance, Keats's (1883) *Ode to Melancholy* is about an emotional state, rather than a totalizing comment on the nature of humanity. It captures a mood and a moment. If art, as Langer (1957) suggests, is the best way we have to represent our feelings, it should come as no surprise that the feelings expressed can be complicated and even contradictory. The perversity of art is its very strength.

The second goal of revision is to communicate our perceptions to the reader exactly as we have experienced them, or as close as we can get. Although we can never know how our work will be understood and taken up, we are always striving for an exactitude of expression. This involves a kind of doubled vision, as the writer strives for critical distance from the work and the feelings it evokes at the same time as staying open to their effect and nuances.

In the popular imagination, the business of writing is seen as imaginative, creative, or a "right-brain" endeavor. In reality, it simultaneously requires the cooperation of the more logical left brain, as the writer works in a clinical way to meet the demands and needs of an imagined audience. The work of beginning writers is typically marred by shorthand accounts that depend on knowledge that the writer has failed to divulge. Often, this background knowledge is so obvious to the author that it has become invisible, like Dillard's bullfrog. The hard work of exactitude is avoided through the use of clichés. Characters are introduced, but we do not know how we should feel about them. If we are suddenly introduced to the narrator's mother, for instance, the information we need is not just factual but relational. The memoirist knows her mother very well, but the reader does not. How does the narrator relate to her mother? What is their history together? What does the reader need to know about her to access the narrative?

This kind of information cannot be baldly presented at the outset of the narrative as an indigestible summary—another common mistake made by those new to the writing process. When readers agree to enter one's fictional world, they suspend disbelief as they buy in to the world created by the text and develop empathy with the characters involved. They do not want to be "told" what to think and feel; they want to figure it out for themselves. Characters must be introduced and scenes created quickly and seamlessly to maintain the reader's belief in the fictional world on offer.

This is difficult, but not as difficult as the achievement of the first goal of revision: simply telling the truth. Here is Dillard (1990, p. 290), again, on this topic:

The interior life is often stupid. Its egoism blinds it and deafens it; its imagination spins out ignorant tales, fascinated. It fancies that the western wind blows on the Self, and leaves fall at the feet of the Self for a reason, and people are watching. A mind risks real ignorance for the sometimes paltry prize of an imagination enriched. The trick of reason is to get the imagination to seize the actual world—if only from time to time.

The fact that one is writing about one's life does not necessarily mean that one understands what happened, only that one is interested in thinking and writing about it. As I suggested in the previous chapter, our understandings will always be partial and incomplete, and they do depend, as Dillard (1990) suggests, on working through the fascinating but ignorant tales our ego offers by way of distraction. In their essay on the nature of learning in poststructural times and the consequent crisis of representation discussed by Denzin (see Chapter 7), Pitt and Britzman (2003) define learning as the abandonment of lovely knowledge—that which makes good sense—in favor of more difficult knowledge. As I have, they suggest that the force of earlier events will always be interpreted through the lens of unresolved psychical conflicts. They speak to the difficulty of constructing meaningful narratives from these unclaimed experiences and the temptation to dance around them, rest in blind spots, or produce narratives that are "satisfying" but essentially inaccurate. In this sense, good writing is not so much about intelligence, the understanding of literary techniques and genres, or the extent of one's vocabulary as it is about one's ability to see honestly and to challenge one's perceptions. This is what makes writing and revision a political and spiritual, as well as an artistic, process.

I do have some advice to offer about how to approach the revision of one's work, but I must predicate it by saying that success will depend upon the kind of emotional and uncompromising honesty that Dillard describes and upon the courage of the writer. There are no short cuts. "There is something that you find interesting, for a reason hard to explain," says Dillard (1990, pp. 24–25). "It's hard to explain because you've never read it on any page; there you begin." *Pilgrim at Tinker Creek* is just that kind of groundbreaking text, breaking down and combining the genres of Thoreau-like journaling, personal essay, and novel, ranging across philosophy, scientific and natural observation, and metaphysical inquiry.

As I remain with Dillard as a model, I begin my advice by drawing attention to the spirit of curiosity she describes. To reread a first draft productively requires a kind of disinterested openness to surprise. In a letter to his brother, Keats (1817, p. 1) called this capacity negative capability, or the ability to rest in "uncertainties, Mysteries, doubts without any reaching after fact and reason." It is a form of openness to learning, a willingness to replace lovely knowledge with more difficult knowledge. For the writer, it can feel like launching from one trapeze without being certain that the next is available and within one's grasp.

The writer must open to the work, which has now become something separate and independent of the writer. "I do not so much write a book as sit up with it, as with a dying friend," says Dillard (2009, p. 581). "During visiting hours," she continues, "I enter its room with dread and sympathy for its many disorders. I hold its hand and hope it will get better." The only question to be considered in this process is, What the work wants from you. What does it want to become? "The writing has changed, in your hands, and in a twinkling, from an expression of your notions to an epistemological tool. The new place interests you because it is not clear. You attend" (Dillard, 2009, p. 549).

There are some strategies that may help, although frankly, they are quite few. The first is to pay attention to the imagery thrown up in the process of the composition of a first draft. If we return for a moment to Freud's (in Phillips, 2006, p. 545) analysis of screen or episodic memories, we can recall that he argued that though they had lain by gold (a deeply affective memory), these memories are not themselves gold, but have lain beside it. "It is a case of displacement along the plane of association by contiguity" he notes, "the replacement of what is repressed by something in its spatial or temporal vicinity" (in Phillips, 2006, p. 545). The imagery in our first drafts can thus be seen as condensed visual maps or images—little suitcases packed with meaning.

Novelist and memoirist Dorothy Allison (1995, pp. 90–94) draws a parallel with hypertext in her memoir *Two or Three Things I Know for Sure*: "Every time you touch a word, a window opens. Behind that word is another story." At the end of this process, her entire life is revealed, and she stands "at the bottom of every story [she] had ever needed to know" (Allison, 1995, p. 94). In my own practice and in assisting others with theirs, I have found that emergent images often seem to know more than the writer about where the work is headed. I have come to call these "guiding" or "controlling" images. Once they have been identified as central, they can be expanded or "pulled through" the work to establish mood and central themes.

In one story, for instance, one of my students wrote about her mother's sudden death. The night her mother died, the narrator was in bed listening to the familiar sounds of her father's nighttime routine in her parents' bedroom above, which ended with his undressing and joining his sleeping wife. On this occasion, one slipper fell to the floor, but not the second, as he turned and realized that his wife lay dead. "You were waiting for the other shoe to drop," murmured one member of the group offering feedback.

The image of the second shoe captured the intention of the piece perfectly, and it became a thread that the writer was able to follow as she revised the piece. It expanded to include its deeper affective purpose—to describe the child narrator's isolation and constant sense of fearful anticipation as a child of unstable parents who constantly bickered, moved from one place and job to another. As she revised, the writer strove for a sense of foreboding and uncertainty in a world incomprehensible and confusion to its childish narrator. The insight also determined the point of view she adopted—a firsthand account by a fallible child narrator with a limited understanding of unfolding events. Once the intention of a piece is discovered, the tone is set for further revision and critique. In this instance, it would not have been productive for those in a feedback circle to ask for things to be made clearer, or explained, as a sense of confusion was the very point of the writing.

It is also necessary to pay attention to the emergent structure of the piece, as one asks what it wants to become. As the writer reads the first draft work, it can be helpful to ask whether it is a poem, a short story, a play, a movie, or a novel. One has to be careful to let go of assumptions here in that one may have *wanted* to write a short story, but the piece does not comply, and trying to wrestle it into a preconceived form is wasted effort. Because the work of revision involves so much uncertainty, following an unproductive direction can lead to confusion and the much-feared phenomenon of writer's block. My (considerable) experience with this ailment leads me to believe that it stems from the very uncertainties described in this chapter.

Some knowledge of craft and genre may be helpful here. A densely imagistic piece may want to be a poem. A piece that depends heavily on dialogue could work as a play. A simply written narrative with a strong message may be productively revised as a parable. A piece with a few main characters, a tight chronology, and a restricted setting sounds like a short story. If so, then what is its narrative arc? If the writer pays attention, he or she will usually be able to identify its rising action, its climactic moment, and its denouement. As Sexton (in Salvio, 2007) has pointed out, the more formal requirements of structure are not empty conventions but a way to channel and illuminate affective content.

Understanding the demands of the craft is not, as I have argued, central to the composition of effective writing. This accessibility is precisely why writing memoir has remained a robust form of social discourse and education. Anyone can write well if they have something important to say, including children, and those with limited access to education, including literary education. That said, paying attention to craft can be a useful distraction. In Chapter 2, I cited Judy Fletcher, who said that the practical details of constructing her memory box took her mind off its difficult affective content. Anything that leads to a state of negative capability or curiosity, rather than rushing to judgment is helpful in this regard. I have found that offering enabling constraints is helpful, particularly in terms of the time allotted for writing, as it removes the ability to think too rationally, to edit (rather than revise), and the ever-present temptation to judge and censor one's work before it is even written. This is why freewriting (discussed in Chapter 6) can be highly effective.

In all these decisions and deliberations, certain questions remain central: What is the work's intention? Have you told the truth? Have you told the whole truth? Is there something that you are holding back, perhaps for later? If so, Dillard (2009, p. 597) has some advice for you:

> Spend it all, shoot it, play it, lose it, all, right away, every time. Do not hoard what seems good for a later place in the book, or for another book; give it, give it all, give it now. The impulse to save something good for a better place later is the signal to spend it now. Something more will arise for later, something better. These things fill from behind, from beneath, like well water. Similarly, the impulse to keep to yourself what you have learned is not only shameful, it is destructive. Anything you do not give freely and abundantly becomes lost to you. You open your safe and find ashes.

References

Allison, D. (1995). *Two or three things I know for sure*. Plume.

Carr, E. (2005). *Growing pains: The autobiography of Emily Carr*. Douglas & McIntyre.

Dillard, A. (1990). *Three by Annie Dillard: Pilgrim at Tinker Creek; An American childhood; The writing life*. Harper Perennial.

Emanuel, L. (1992). In praise of malice: Thoughts on revision. In R. Behn & C. Twichell (Eds.), *The practice of poetry* (pp. 251–256). Quill.

Keats, J. (1817). *Letter to his brothers*. Retrieved July 19, 2020 from mason.gmu.edu/-rnanian/ Keats-NegativeCapability.html

Keats, J. (1883). *The poetical works of John Keats* (Vol. 2). Reeves and Turner.

Langer, S. K. (1957). *Problems of art*. Scribner.

Phillips, A. (Ed.). (2006). *The Penguin Freud reader*. Penguin.

Pitt, A., & Britzman, D. (2003). Speculations on qualities of difficult knowledge in teaching and learning: an experiment in psychoanalytic research. *Qualitative Studies in Education, 16*(6), 755–776.

Robson, C., & Sumara, D. (2007–2009). *OWLS research transcripts of discussions* [Unpublished raw data]. University of British Columbia, Vancouver, BC.

Salvio, P. M. (2007). *Anne Sexton: Teacher of weird abundance*. State University of New York Press.

Tillinghast, R. (2001). Household economy, ruthless romance, and the art of hospitality. In R. Behn & C. Twichell (Eds.), *The practice of poetry* (pp. 245–248). Quill.

CHAPTER NINE

Feedback

IN THIS PART, I suggest that individual acts of perception are partial in all senses of that word: incomplete, biased, and influenced by our desires. For this reason, our ability to see what is in front of us is limited by what we have already seen, what we already know, and what we expect from the future. In this final chapter of Part III, I move our discussion back into the realm of collective learning, as I consider how our limited individual understandings of our histories can be supported and strengthened by the insights and suggestions of others. After all, we are highly social creatures, who invented language as a way to share, discuss, and improve our ideas, values, and knowledge. Without language, we would be trapped in our individual understandings of the world, and we would have a limited collective memory of our culture.

Although discourse, including texts of all kinds, can open us to vital social knowledge, it can also serve to close us down, as it congeals and reproduces the practices of the day. Gee (1990, p. 142) has likened popular discourse to a "social identity kit . . . complete with instructions." In diverse and complex cultures, minorities and less privileged populations (historically, these have included enslaved and racialized others, those who are differently abled, women, genderqueers, queers, immigrants, and the poor) are often excluded and ignored in these totalizing narratives. For this reason, civil rights movements have often focused on lending voice to the marginalized so that they can speak back to oppression and power. The work of critical pedagogue Paulo Freire stands as an example of how the work of learning collectives can break the culture of silence and reestablish "paths of thought that lead to a language of critique" (Giroux, 2001, p. 80).

In constructing these learning collectives, it is important to create pedagogical structures that decenter teaching practices, afford equal access to all participants, and pay close attention to the operations of power, and it is to these topics that I turn our attention next.

In Chapter 5, I wrote about how my class of university students confessed that they did not enjoy group work. They were also quite critical of peer critique and peer grading, which they regarded as a rather specious tip of the hat to democracy in a far-from-democratic context. "We're not going to downgrade our fellow students," said one, "whatever we think of their work." Even in the less grade-oriented milieu of the community arts collective, there are major challenges to the work of peer critiques, many of which can easily become laissez-faire free-for-alls, in which vocal participants strive to assert their opinions (often overly directive), talk about the issues that are suggested in the work, their own experiences with these, or other artistic representations of the issues (such as books or films on the same topic). Artists become confused by conflicting advice, as people suggest, for instance, that the work is too obvious or that it is quite the opposite. Such opposing positions are vigorously defended, almost as a form of verbal sport (Ping-Pong comes to mind), while the artist desperately makes notes or quietly ignores their suggestions or even becomes so confused that they lose clarity on the piece. "Even in consciousness-raising groups," Haug (1992, p. 19) lamented, "everyone sits waiting for her turn and would far rather talk than listen."

In Part I, I discussed Haug's critical writing collectives, in which women helped each other to "hear what has not been said," and "to see things that have not been displayed" (1992, p. 25) using forms of critique that Haug described as "a special kind of detective work. Haug has detailed her methods of working quite precisely in her (2000) piece *Memory-Work as a Method of Social Science Research: A Detailed Rendering of Memory-Work Method*. In the first phase of work, she had people write individually, following simple guidelines (similar to those I described in Chapter 1). The stories were limited to one or two pages and written in the third person (for the authors to achieve psychic distance). The scene was described in as much detail as possible, even if the details seemed inconsequential to the authors, who were encouraged to "describe" the scene rather than to "explain" it.

In the second phase of the work, each member of the group expressed opinions and ideas about each written memory in turn, as the collective looked for similarities and differences between the memories and elements that connected them. Each member identified clichés, generalizations, contradictions, cultural imperatives, and metaphors because these are ways of identifying messages that we take for granted. The group then discussed theories, popular conceptions, sayings, and images that came to mind around the topic being discussed. They also examined what was not written about in the memory (but might be expected to have been expressed) because Haug believed that such silences can point to issues of significance, issues that may be painful or problematic for the author. These are excellent suggestions that might be taken up by any group looking to engage in critique that is emancipatory in its intention.

Table 9.1 shows a copy of the worksheet that Haug (2000) offered as a way to record the process and outcomes of collective editing.

Table 9.1: Haug's Worksheet for Collective Feedback

Initial thesis statement of author's meaning:						
Common sense theory:						
Analysis of elements of language:						
List of verbs as activity	Linguistic peculiarities	Emotion	Motivation	Others presented in narrative	Vacuums	Contradictions

Haug's (2000) rigorous methodological focus on the use of language was taken up by members of the feminist collective biography project convened by Bronwyn Davies and Susanne Gannon (2006), who invited a group of colleagues together to investigate the topic of girlhood, drawing on Haug's methodology. Their work together involved "the writing and . . . analysis of remembered stories written by the researchers themselves" (2006, p. 4) and the disruption of these stories as they were critiqued in the light of feminist theory. This second text also offers valuable suggestions as to how the work can be conducted, as well as its challenges. I highly recommend it.

Crucially, both Haug's work and that of Davies and Gannon (2006) were conducted primarily with small groups of educated academic feminists. Perhaps for this reason, these authors are rather vague when it comes to the exact agreements and pedagogies they negotiated around the management of discussions and critiques. If we apply Haug's method of examining the author's choice of verb to her own article, we find that she often retreats into the pseudoscientific detachment of the passive voice. Actions take place, but we do not know who initiated them, as in the following instance (2000, p. 9): "Some of the theoretical assumptions of memory-work should be explained before working with the remembered scenes . . ." Who will, or who should, assume this leadership role? Haug is strangely silent on the matter of who was "in charge" of the work in hand. At some points, it seems clear that she directed most of the work conducted. At other times, she talks about a collective process but offers no detail regarding how, and how often, this was conducted. At other times, she mentions the existence of "team leaders" but fails to discuss their remit and role.

I suspect, that like Davies and Gannon's (2006) research, Haug's work throughout the years leaned heavily on the existing traditions of the academy, which, like all powerful institutions, comes complete with its own hierarchical structures of power and established ways of operating, including pedagogical systems. This reality is richly acknowledged by Davies and her colleagues: "Writing stories was also a time when I felt that I had forgotten to wear my knickers to school," says one of the graduate students (2006, p. 140) as she recalls her sense of being overawed by the presence of her professors "doing day-to-day things and talking about tragic relationships." Another says:

> I know that writing this may upset you Bronwyn but here goes anyway: I always knew that you were in control. There was no way that you would allow a piece of writing to go to a journal with your name on it that you weren't happy with. (2006, p. 143)

Davies and Gannon's seamlessly coauthored text rightly includes many references to these unequal distributions of social and academic capital, inequalities that become crucial in projects aimed at liberation and emancipation.

Although many liberal educators, such as I, have fled from the halls of formal education to less traditional sites of community education (Sandlin, 2010), we have not escaped the operations of power. The fact that I have a doctorate, that I am an adjunct professor, that my writing has been published, and that I occupied a leadership position in the group for many years did afford me considerable status in Quirk-e and still does in other groups I facilitate. As facilitator of much of the group's process and as an editor of many of our publications, I also have the power to forefront or ignore someone's artwork or single them out for praise—forms of power that are not negligible. That said, I do not have the power to dispense grades, funding, or invitations to conferences and joint publications, as senior academics do. The workshops are free, and attendance is voluntary. There are no penalties (other than my disapproval and that of other members of the group) for incomplete work, late arrival, or poor attendance.

For the first four years of our work together, we concentrated on product rather than process, as we strove to establish our presence in the community by producing and showing our artwork. In 2010, however, we reached a crossroads in terms of giving and receiving feedback. A vocal subset of the group (four or five people) become impatient with our protocols for critique, which were admittedly fairly loose at that point because we had never taken the time to consider them closely. I was, after all, used to a model in which the facilitator was the most important critic. This particular group of writers saw themselves (with some justification) as "good writers" who were highly committed, and they believed that "telling it like it is" would be more productive than being restrained and polite. Underlying their discourse was a desire to get published or, at least, to fit into the local culture of established writers. They wanted rigorous, unfiltered, "professional" feedback on their work and had become impatient with social niceties.

Their attitude upset some members of the collective, including some who had suffered from trauma. These members said that this new, more "professional" approach to critique created a competitive and hostile environment in which they did not feel safe. They espoused a more "nurturing" approach to feedback, one in which difficult emotional content was acknowledged and discussed with care and attention to the writer who had disclosed it. They were less concerned about getting published or improving the quality of their writing and more concerned about the ways in which the writing opened discussion of some of the sociopolitical dimensions of their writing. They were process-oriented rather than product-oriented.

This disagreement became problematic quite quickly. Tears were shed, and harsh words were uttered. Finally, I decided to intervene, which I did by first holding a discernment process (see Chapter 5). As we talked, it became clear that the conflict was not just about the practicalities and etiquette of group feedback but also its deep purpose and how this might reflect our core values. Clearly, we had not discussed these sufficiently.

I return here, briefly, to Oliver (2001), who notes that address-ability and response-ability are the roots of subjectivity and that they can be damaged by oppression and subordination. "Witnessing," she argues, "works to ameliorate the trauma particular to othered subjectivity. This is because witnessing is the essential dynamic of all subjectivity, its constitutive event and process" (2001, p. 7). She also goes on to suggest that those who have been oppressed have a particular desire to be recognized (and, ironically, to be recognized by their oppressors). However, when such recognition is seen as being conferred by the dominant group that oppressed them, their need can easily throw them back into the hierarchy of domination and master–slave relationships. Oliver's work serves to remind us of both the potential of recognizing the emotional content of our work and the risks involved. This is not just a practical question, although it does have practical implications for our pedagogy. It is a question of intention, and it was to that shared intention that I turned the focus of the debate. I invited the whole collective, not just the members of the "two factions," to set all their other work aside and take the time to discuss our feelings and ideas (and histories) about critique and reach some kind of consensus about what might work best.

I began by asking them to brainstorm what they had liked and disliked about the group critiques they had experienced. They were quite passionate in their responses, some of which surprised all of us. For instance, like many others in the collective, I had not thought too much about the significance of a nonresponse to work shared, but several members commented that they often interpreted silence as a negative response that carried more weight than even spoken compliments. Many people wanted a critical distance to be set between the writer and the writing. They did not appreciate "nosey" requests for personal information beyond the scope of the piece under review (for instance, "Did you ever make things right with your mother?"). They didn't enjoy a "pack mentality" around critique, in which perceived "leaders" set the tone for comment. This led us to find ways in which everyone's first impression could be laid out early on (see the "Quick Hits" later in the chapter).

Above all, we found that the kind of feedback that worked for everyone (including our two warring groups) came from a place of advocacy for the work. As we shared our feelings about people who talked too much, people who were overly directive, people who digressed, and people who were harsh in their written comments, we realized that these behaviors were ego-driven. Just as we must move beyond the ego in seeing "what happened" and writing honestly about it, so we must move beyond our own tastes and predilections in responding to the work of others. The central question is always, *What does this work want to be?* Other questions will stem from the answer. The question, *Do I like this work?* hardly matters.

Finally, we agreed that writers are highly sensitive—even the more experienced of us could be easily triggered by a single remark. Many of our suggestions, which follow, were generated by the horror stories people shared—about people who began feedback sessions by offering grammatical corrections, people who surreptitiously checked their iPhones during discussions, or people who made moral judgments of characters in the work.

The following is the end result of our conversation: a set of negotiated guidelines for giving and receiving feedback. Clearly, they did not emerge in such an organized way. Our note-takers listed the main points of conversations held over the course of three weeks. I organized these into a schema, circulated the results for further feedback, and refined the schema in the light of these additional comments (see Table 9.2 below).

Table 9.2: General Guidelines for Giving Feedback

General Guidelines for Giving Feedback
Please bear the following in mind during all sessions:
• It doesn't matter whether or not you like the work. What matters is what the author and the work itself want it to be. We are advocates for that.
• Start positive. It's important for the author to know what works.
• Stay *something*. Silence can be distressing.
• Separate the narrator from the author. Don't ask or assume if work is autobiographical.

- Don't digress. Particularly about how this reminds you of something you read/or that happened to you. Save those thoughts for later, informal discussion.
- Leave the rewriting itself to the author, unless she asks for specific suggestions.
- Your job is to strengthen the work, not score points.

Some useful methods for giving feedback

- Quick Hits. Go around the circle and have each person give an overview of his/her response in 30 seconds or so. See if an interesting point emerges to guide the discussion from then on in.
- Free for All. Just wait to see what people say. Free-form discussion.
- Response to a Question. Either the author or someone in the group frames a key question, which the group begins the discussion with this.
- Set formula. The group can work through set questions.

  Examples:
  - What worked for me. What are my questions? What are my suggestions for improvement?
  - What is the gift of this piece?
  - Pretend you wrote the piece, then fill in this blank. When I wrote this piece, I was . . .
- Author led discussion. The author says what his/her needs and questions are, and leads the group with them.

Key decisions for facilitation

- How long does each writer have?
- How will you keep the discussion on track? (use of a code word or phrase: "Be that as it may, let us move on . . .")
- Will the author listen in silence, or participate in the discussion?

Responsibilities

The writer

- ❖ Distribute clear copies, double spaced and with numbered pages.
- ❖ Try not be apologetic about your piece, or issue disclaimers.
- ❖ You may wish to say nothing about the piece, so as to elicit unprejudiced responses.
- ❖ You may instead wish to provide a little context, along the following lines:
  - Is the piece near completion or a work in progress, "stand-alone" or part of a longer project?
  - What are your own feelings about it?
  - Is there any information the reader needs to access the piece?
  - What kind of feedback do you want—answers to specific questions or general responses?
  - Is there feedback you don't want? Some writers welcome picky line edits for example and some detest them. It's your responsibility to be clear about your priorities.

❖ Be clear whether you wish just to listen to and absorb responses offered or whether you prefer to participate in the conversation. Both have merit, but in either case, try not to justify or explain too much or too quickly. It's often more useful to listen as someone else does this. "What did everyone else think?" is a useful question here.

❖ If you start to feel defensive or upset, try to let the group or person know.

The reader

❖ Make notes of the writer's requests. (I find it most useful to do so on the front page of the manuscript.)

❖ Read the work with the diligence, care, and respect you would like someone to bring to reading yours.

❖ Make frequent marginal comments. (There's nothing worse than no response or minimal response.) If you liked something, put a check mark or a smiley face or a word or two of praise ("funny" "loved this" "well put" "fresh image"). Emotional reactions can be useful too ("Oh my God!" "I'm in suspense" "What a nightmare"). Too often we highlight problems and forget to show what we liked or felt.

❖ Try not to be snippy. If you were confused, say so. If you have problems, make a note of them, but avoid multiple exclamation marks, sarcastic or brusque comments.

❖ Don't feel that you have to have to justify all your remarks. You may have a response that you can't fully explain. Note it anyway. It may promote useful discussion.

❖ Write a detailed endnote that summarizes your response to the piece. Start with the positive and end on suggestions that might take the work further.

❖ Start with the positive and the important comments, work through to suggestions for change and leave small 'picky' points to the end.

❖ Try to be an advocate for the work, to help it to be the best it can, to work with the author's intention. Avoid the temptation to rewrite the piece the way you want it to be.

❖ Separate the writer from the protagonist when you talk (i.e. say "the protagonist" or "the narrator" rather than "you"). Even if you know they are one and the same, the distinction will help to maintain objectivity and emotional distance.

❖ Remember that you can check in with the writer if you're worried about his/her feelings ("Are you OK with this?" "Does this feel right/helpful?").

❖ Try to remember your first response, even if it's different from everyone else's. It can be useful for a group to take a "quick hit" from each member, before opinions merge.

❖ Always invite the writer to make a final comment

Remember the Big Picture

In this kind of collective critique, the most useful questions include these:

• What is trying to emerge in the work?

• What images and phrases have the most energy? Where, if anywhere, does this energy flag?

• What form and shape does the work seem to strive for? Is it dense and imagistic like a poem? Does it have the narrative arc of a short story? Might the preponderance of dialogue and action offer theatrical potential?

• What feelings does the work evoke? What grabbed your attention?

• What could be usefully unpacked in the work? In other words, has the writer skipped across difficult material or hidden it under clichés or half-truths?

—Claire Robson & the Quirk-e Collective, 2010

These guidelines serve one single aim: to strengthen the work and to position the author as the prime agent in the process, thus countering the patriarchal power dynamic in which writers are subjected to the group. Most important, they forefront the work and its intention. Knee-jerk reactions are discouraged as participants are constantly reminded that their opinions about the work are less important than the intention of the work itself. As we proceeded with our work together, our shared contract for offering and receiving feedback proved to be an invaluable reference point.

In later work, we were able to become more sophisticated. The following worksheet offers an instance of more theoretical and critical analysis, drawn from Gee's (1990) work on discourse analysis. We used it not so much in giving feedback on each other's work, but it proved useful in analyzing the archival texts and documents we considered as we worked on our anthology *The Bridge Generation* (Robson & Blair, 2014).

Quirk-e's Discourse Analysis Toolkit

The Subject Tool.

Why did the writer choose this subject? What is s/he saying about it? Have other important subjects been ignored?

The Making Things Strange Tool.

Try to imagine that you are from another culture or planet. What would you find confusing or strange about this piece? What might you not understand?

The Information Tool.

What information is being offered in the piece? Where is it from and how is it sourced? What is being left out?

The Fill-In Tool.

What do we 'fill in' ourselves to make sense of the piece? What assumptions lie behind it?

The Language Tool.

How is language being used, and why? What kinds of words does the writer choose? What is the tone and mood of the piece?

The Topic Flow Tool.
What are the steps in the argument? Why are ideas presented in this particular order?

The Doing and Not Saying Tool.
What is the writer trying to *do* in the piece, without necessarily *saying* it?

The Identities Tool.
How does the author present him/herself? What identity is s/he trying to enact? How is the writer trying to position others?

The World Tool.
What kind of world is the writer trying to promote? What is being valued?

The Politics Tool.
Who is seen to have power and goods? Who is left out? What political ends does the piece serve?

Adapted by Claire Robson from James Paul Gee's (2010) book: *How to Do Discourse Analysis*

The guidelines offered in this chapter worked well for this group, and hopefully, they will have value, at least as a starting point, for other groups seeking to engage in this work. Clearly, they are not offered as an exemplar, but rather as an example of good practice.

As the writer follows her trail of words to find their intention, there are few rules and no objective measure of the truth and value of our words. Even consensus cannot help the individual writer follow her way toward clarity and truth of expression. This can be a challenge, particularly in a world that has taught us to seek authority. However, those of us who work against the grain, it can be freeing as it opens up the possibility of productive resistance to dominant narratives.

In Part IV, I turn our attention to this possibility. Chapter 10 focuses on possible genres, outcomes, and venues for creative expression and their respective potential for social change. It will be illustrated through three arts collaborations between queer youth and elders: a book, a theatrical show, and a project whose outcomes were digital video and posters. Chapter 11 focuses on the maxim "show, don't tell" as it revisits the difference between re-presenting a scene as opposed to "telling about what I felt." Chapter 12 pulls together the threads of the book's exploration of the ethics of representation.

References

Davies, B., & Gannon, S. (Eds.). (2006). *Doing collective biography*. Open University Press.

Gee, J.P. (2010). *How to do discourse analysis: A toolkit*. Routledge.

Gee, J. P. (1990). *Social linguistics and literacies: Ideology in discourses, critical perspectives on literacy and education*. Falmer Press.

Giroux, H. A. (2001). Culture, power and transformation in the work of Paulo Freire. In F. Schultz (Ed.), *SOURCES: Notable selections in education* (3rd ed., pp. 77–86). McGraw Hill Dushkin.

Haug, F. (1992). *Beyond female masochism: Memory work and politics*. Verso.

Haug, F. (2000). *Memory-work as a method of social science research, a detailed rendering of memory work method*. http://www.friggahaug.inkrit.de/documents/memorywork-researchguidei7.pdf

Oliver, K. (2001). *Witnessing: beyond recognition*. University of Minnesota Press.

Robson, C., & Blair, K. (Eds.). (2014). *The bridge generation*. Lulu.

Sandlin, J. A., Schultz, B. D., & Burdick, J. (2010). *Handbook of public pedagogy: Education and learning beyond schooling*. Routledge.

PART IV

REPRESENTING

CHAPTER TEN

Show. Don't Tell

It is the function of art to reorganize experience so it is perceived freshly. At the very least, the painting, or the poem, or the play cleanses a familiar scene, washing away the film of habit and dust collected over time so that it is seen anew. When it is most radical, the work of art draws the viewer to it, engaging expectations, memories, recognitions, and simultaneously interrupts the viewer's customary response, contradicting expectations with new possibilities, violating memories, displacing recognition with estrangement.

—Grumet (1988, p. 81)

GRUMET'S DEFINITION OF THE function of art takes us into this next part, in which I consider artistic representations, through which the artist attempts to present again (or re-present), an event that has already occurred. As Grumet implies, artistic representations often interrupt, rather than confirm, our understandings; they can never represent those events as they actually occurred because our perceptions are clouded by the customary film of habit and expectations. The "actual" does not exist, in a practical, if not a philosophical, sense. However hard we search after meaning or try to communicate *what happened*, the best we can do is to represent our *experiences* of what happened because "the thing can never speak for itself." When we make art, we do so in the hope that the reader or audience will let go of what they expect to see to experience it anew and see it through our eyes. Simultaneously, we acknowledge that language cannot ever represent even our experiences of events directly and exactly. As Merleau-Ponty (in Johnson, 1994, p. 82) put it, "like the weaver, the writer works on the wrong side of his material. He has only to do with the language, and it is thus that he suddenly finds himself surrounded by sense."

Annie Dillard (1990, pp. 549–550) calls the line of words that the writer composes "a miner's pick, a woodcarver's gouge, a surgeon's probe" that digs a path we follow. She reminds us that this path can change in a twin-kling, and as we make artistic choices, we find ourselves in "new territories" as the choices we have made determine the range of choices next available. In the same essay cited earlier, Merleau-Ponty (in Johnson, 1994, p. 247) describes watching a slow-motion film of Matisse painting and seeing his brush hover as he considered and discarded various artistic choices on the "still open whole of the painting" before bringing his brush to the line that called for it "in order that the painting might finally be that which it was in the process of becoming."

Although most of us believe that other people have interior lives, this is not a given, only a theory. Indeed, the notion of consciousness as it is gen-erally understood is fairly new. Although the relics of even the earliest hu-mans show that they had spiritual beliefs, and thus presumably believed in interiority, we did not develop a working theory of consciousness until the mid-17th century, with the work of Descartes (*I think, therefore I am*) and Locke (Van Gulig, 2018). As may be imagined, ideas and discussions about the nature of consciousness, mind, or identity have generated a rich body of research, both qualitative and quantitative. These debates do not concern us here. A simple understanding of the Theory of Mind—the belief that others are animated by mental states that differ from our own—will suffice.

Our sense of what is happening in the world is the result of the complex interpretations we process as we perceive and, simultaneously, create mean-ing from our perceptions. Without even being aware of it, we constantly and effortlessly make sense of gestures and behaviors, such as a raised hand, or a smile. In his essay "How to Recognize a Poem," Fish (cited in Zunshine, 2006, p. 275) demonstrates this with an example drawn from one of his classrooms:

> While I was in the course of vigorously making a point, one of my students, William Newlin by name, was just as vigorously waving his hand. When I asked the other members of the class what it was that [he] was doing, they all answered that he was seeking permission to speak. I then asked them how they knew that. The immediate reply was that it was obvious; what else could he be thought of doing? The meaning of his gesture, in other words, was right there on its surface, available for reading by anyone who had the eyes to see.

Fish is careful to point out, however, that this meaning was highly contextual and

> would not have been available to someone without any knowledge of what
> was involved in being a student. Such a person might have thought that
> Mr. Newlin was pointing to the fluorescent lights hanging from the ceiling,
> or calling our attention to some object that was about to fall ("the sky is
> falling," "the sky is falling"). And if the someone in question were a child
> of elementary or middle-school age, Mr. Newlin might well have been seen
> as seeking permission not to speak but to go to the bathroom, an inter-
> pretation or reading that would never have occurred to a student at Johns
> Hopkins or any other institution of "higher learning."

As I take this theory into our topic here—the field of art—I draw further on the work of cognitive literary theorist Lisa Zunshine (2006), who has reminded us that trying to figure out what others are thinking and feeling is so integral and so fundamental to the state of being human that we are scarcely aware that we are doing it. She also suggests that our ancestors developed these processes of "mind reading" thousands of years ago (probably in the Pleistocene period) because to survive, it was necessary to make sense of the behaviors of others in their group.

Throughout her book on *Witnessing*, Oliver (2001, p. 3) argues that our understandings of subjectivity lie at the foundation of what we believe about ourselves and the world. To see people as *the other* or as objects alienates us from both ourselves and others and allows the dehumanization that leads to oppression. To see address-ability and response-ability as the roots of subjectivity can help us take a step toward "repairing subjectivity as we take up the positions of speaking subjects" (Oliver, 2001, p. 7). Ian McEwan wrote (in Lodge, 2002, p. 42) "Imagining what it is like to be someone other than yourself is at the core of our humanity. It is the essence of compassion and the beginning of morality." This kind of imagining, the business of walking in someone else's shoes, is called empathy.

Zunshine (2006) goes on to suggest that Theory of Mind offers an important reason for our historic attraction to artistic representations—they are entertaining for sure, but they also engage us in the practice of mind reading or empathetic skills that are crucial to our happiness and survival.

And, as Oliver (2001) suggests, recognition by others means that our experiences have been *witnessed*—we have been seen and acknowledged in a profound and intimate way. The skills required for empathetic understandings include interpreting motivations: keeping track of who said what, when, and with what level of credibility. Here, Zunshine (2006, p. 5) draws on another theoretical concept: metarepresentation, which she calls "source monitoring." Much of the information we rely on in our quotidian existence is so soundly and multiply sourced (for instance, "the world is round") that it can be taken as read. Other information is processed for validity as we make metarepresentational judgments about the reliability of its source. Zunshine (2006, p. 26) posits that books are nothing less than "a thousands'-year-long experimentation with our cognitive adaptations"; they provide a daily workout for our Theory of Mind and our ability to weigh the truth values of what the characters tell us, through their speech and actions. As the novelist David Lodge (2002, p. 10) has put it, the novel is "man's most successful effort to describe the experience of individual human beings moving through space and time."

These theories have clear implications for the processes of artistic representations, in general, and the field of memoir, in particular, since the focus of this genre is the dense specificity of personal experience. Memoirs are always unique because each of us has a very different personal history, and the creation of literary texts recapitulates this uniqueness. Jane Austen's *Emma*, for example, could not have been written by anybody else and never will be written by anyone else again. An experiment demonstrating the second law of thermodynamics is, and must be, repeatable by any competent scientist.

As Varela (1999) has said, consciousness is grounded in concrete activity. Sumara (2002) has shown how our sense of who we are is sustained in the quotidian by the context we create in our homes and through the artifacts we have collected. By writing about these things—houses and pets, brooches, photographs, and countryside—the writer cannot help but write about him- or herself. More important, the writer cannot tell the reader directly what he or she felt but must somehow re-present the experiences that generated those feelings in the hope that the reader will experience them as well. Most practicing writers (Dillard, 1990; Shields, 2002; Winterson, 1995) agree that we can both re-experience and re-present the subtleties of our own experiences and those of others through rendering the details of lived experiences. "My task, which I am trying to achieve," Joseph Conrad (2006, para 4) wrote in the preface to one of his tales, "is by the power of the written word to make you hear, to make you feel—it is before all, to make you see. That—and no more, and it is everything." The importance of representing the "embodied details" of the scenes presented by writers is something that Haug (2000, p. 12) stresses throughout her essay on methods.

Cognitive scientists use the word *qualia* (singular, *quale*) to describe the details of lived experience. The novelist David Lodge (2002, p. 8) describes them this way: "Examples of qualia are the smell of freshly ground coffee or the taste of pineapple; such experiences have a distinctive phenomenological character which we have all experienced but which, it seems, is very difficult to describe." They are, by nature, subjective and qualitative as they attempt to describe "what it is like" to smell coffee or see a flower. They can be sense data (such as sight or smell), either real or imagined, as well as bodily sensations, such as pain or hunger, and feelings or moods, such as boredom or anger.

Successful writers are able to delineate "the specific nature of our subjective experiences in the world" (Lodge, 2002, p. 8) by representing (re-presenting) such qualia as the smell of coffee or the red fog of rage. In memoir, as much as in fiction, it is in the reconstruction and the reading of these specific details that we come closest to sharing our lived experience with others. The work of the artist then is to "take the reader there" by re-creating events by re-presenting the elements of a scene. When we read good writing, whether it's poetry, prose, or play, we feel like we're actually there, experiencing the scene firsthand. Good writers "show, rather than tell," and they create intimate work that draws readers in. There is a crucial difference, as Ayn Rand (2000) points out, between narration and dramatization. To dramatize something is to show it as if it were happening before the reader's eyes so that he or she is in the position of an observer at the scene. To narrate, by contrast, is to synopsize: You tell the reader about something that has happened, but you do not let him be a witness. Writers must show, not tell; they must take the reader there, and this they achieve through the reproduction of as many as possible of the qualia that made up the original experience.

This may seem obvious, but it is a conclusion central to the successful memoir, and it is a lesson that new writers often find difficult, as they struggle to represent their experiences. The temptation is to "tell" the reader what happened or overload the piece with adjectives. One member of the

Quirk-e collective, Gayle Roberts, was one such writer. She joined the group at its inception in 2006, largely because she felt it was important to share her experiences in transitioning from someone perceived as male (Michael) to the woman (Gayle) whom she had long felt was her authentic identity. A retired physics teacher, Gayle was intelligent, well read, and in possession of excellent skills as far as writing nonfiction was concerned. Indeed, she had worked on several educational texts and books about trans* experiences. Gayle was very determined to turn her hand to writing memoir and quite used to being successful in anything she set her mind to in this way. However, for this self-described "left-brained, scientific" person, understanding the difference among narration, exposition, and telling, on one hand, and fictionalizing, dramatizing, and showing, on the other, was a major, and often frustrating, challenge.

With Gayle's permission, I share an example of her early writing from one of the Quirk-e Collective's early anthologies:

> I was just about at my breaking point trying to cope with my increasingly painful feelings of wanting to be a woman and trying to hide them from my friends, students, teacher-colleagues, and school administrators. Even teaching no longer enabled me to escape briefly those awful feelings as it had done in the past. I was at the lowest point in my life. I knew I had to transition for peace of mind, but was afraid to do so. Would I, like so many of my transsexual friends, lose everything that was meaningful to me—my friends, career, and, most importantly, my wife? (Gayle Roberts, 2007, excerpt from Deep Pockets, *Transformations*)

As I critiqued this piece, I felt considerable sympathy for its protagonist and applauded her courage in writing about this time. However, I had to point out that it is a classic example of telling, rather than showing, in several regards. It depends on clichés ("at my breaking point"), bald statements of feeling ("at the lowest point of my life"), and adjectives ("awful," "increasingly painful") to explain what the protagonist felt. Although other people (colleagues, friends, and the protagonist's wife) are mentioned as being emotionally significant, we do not 'meet' them in the piece. Finally, it uses a rhetorical question, often used (unsuccessfully, as here) by beginning writers to generate a sense of suspense and drama. When I offered Gayle this feedback, she responded by email.

Hi Claire:

Many thanks for today. I have attached the revised version of my story Visits with Mother.

I have also attached a question. I am very confused about something which I hope I have made clear in the second attachment. I hope you are able to give me an answer because at the moment I feel that unless I resolve it, my writing is not going to improve.

Many thanks Claire.

Gayle

The question that Gayle asked was about this crucial distinction between showing and telling. Gayle wanted to know how on earth she could "show" her experiences when she went through them alone. It is an important question because it goes to the kind of claustrophobic interiority of many memoirs: the tendency to "stay in the author's head" and write directly about the thoughts and feelings that occurred there. Here is my response:

Hi Gayle,

As I think I already said (I hope so), you've done a wonderful job with the story. It reads so much more tightly. I realize that I didn't address your other questions though. I do think that they are useful for us all to consider, and, with your permission, I'd like to talk about this in the workshop—if we have time, on Wednesday (and if not, the week after).

A good first question to ask yourself might be why, exactly, you feel that you cannot "show" what you were experiencing. You say that this is because you went through this alone, and no one saw you, and I'm sure that's partly true. But you still had experiences—looked in shop windows, read magazines, watched TV—and all of these reflected images of what a woman should be. Also, you visited doctors, therapists, talked to some friends, negotiated the change with colleagues. There is always stuff to show—even when we are completely isolated.

I suspect that the problem is this . . . words cannot begin to explain how you felt. You want to communicate that to the reader—but you can't. You feel it is too painful, too difficult. But there again—you have no other choice, and no other option except words.

If we analyze what you did below, we can actually break it down:

1) to use emotional language "emotionally difficult," "anguish," "awful," "I felt alienated," "deep inner peace"

2) to tell us how impossible it is to describe what's going on "I have no words to describe it"

3) to use imagery—"flooding" and the extended "actor" and "prisoner" images

The first two don't work too well. You can use them sparingly at best, and you have to "earn" them first. You have to establish the feeling before you get the right to state it this baldly. Ditto the second. I know it's tempting, Gayle, but you simply cannot address this emotional material head on.

You are best off with the images. They have some energy and currency, but the images need to be much more developed.

I will try to find some examples of work that deal with difficult emotional material effectively, and bring them along so we can analyze them a little.

Thanks for raising this. It's important to everyone in the group!

Claire

We discussed the issue as a collective during our next session, drawing on examples from our own work and those of practicing artists, including the following extract from Patricia Highsmith's (1952, p. 6) novel *The Price of Salt* as an example of the use of qualia:

The lunch hour in the coworkers' cafeteria at Frankenberg's had reached its peak. There was no room left at any of the long tables, and more and more people were arriving to wait back of the wooden barricades by the cash register. People who had already got their trays of food wandered about between the tables in search of a spot they could squeeze into, or a place that somebody was about to leave, but there was no place. The roar of dishes, chairs, voices, shuffling feet, and the bra-a-ack of the turnstiles in the bare-walled room was like the din of a single huge machine. Therese ate nervously, with the "Welcome to Frankenberg's" booklet propped up in front of her against a sugar container. She had read the thick booklet through last week, in the first day of training class, but she had nothing else with her to read, and in the coworkers' cafeteria, she felt it necessary to concentrate on something. So she read again about vacation benefits, the three weeks' vacation given to people who had worked fifteen years at Frankenberg's, and she ate the hot plate special of the day—a grayish slice of roast beef with a ball of mashed potatoes covered with brown gravy, a heap of peas, and a tiny paper cup of horseradish.

Gayle wrote to me again after the workshop:

Hi Claire:

I woke up this morning with a mini epiphany (or is it an epiphanette?).

I have been somewhat frustrated at not getting on with my memoir. Part of the reason for not doing anything has been because I didn't know how to deal with all the emotionally painful episodes in my life—first marriage, gender dysphoria etc. etc. I realized this morning that my difficulty is related to what you and I have discussed through emails and what you covered in class on Wednesday. I realize now I didn't have the right "tools" to continue my memoir. I believe I have them now but recognize I don't yet know how to use them effectively. I need time to use them and when I feel I have mastered them, or at least used them successfully a few times, I can retackle my memoir. I don't feel bad now for leaving it as I realize my skills need to develop some more before I return to it.

Thought I would let you know this. It's also another way for me to say thank you again for helping me grow some more.

All the best.

Gayle

Although it took Gayle a while to master the tools of representation, she did so very successfully. One of her stories has been published in the Arsenal Pulp Press anthology, *First Person Queer* (Labonte & Schimel, 2007), which won a Lambda Literary Award in 2008, and an Independent Publisher Award (Gold) in the same year. Another piece was made into a film by artists in Toronto. Gayle is currently working with great confidence on her full-length memoir. I take the liberty here of concluding this chapter by reproducing one of Gayle's short stories, "The Girl in the Pond." It was the first major breakthrough in Gayle's writing in terms of its ability to stay out of the editorial voice, its sparing use of adjectives, and the profound pathos it incites in the reader through sharp physical detail and the careful construction of a narrative arc.

> "Remember, Michael, don't let go of my hand," my mother cautioned me as the crowd surged forward towards the edge of the platform. The train belched black smoke and white steam as it entered the station, and I felt her hand tightening as she pulled me towards the opening coach doors. Soldiers, sailors, and airmen flooded out of the coaches, dropped their kitbags, and swept their wives and children into their arms.
>
> As my mother pulled me around one of the celebrating families who blocked our path, my attention changed from the coaches to the man. He was wearing an army uniform and could easily have been my father. He was big even though he was kneeling down with his arms wrapped around his daughter. He kissed her tenderly on the cheek, supported her in the crook of his arm and then stood up. With his other arm, he pulled his wife towards him and the three of them embraced. The soldier's daughter was about my age and, like me, had probably just started school as she was wearing a gray pleated skirt with matching knee-high socks and a green jacket which had a crest on the breast pocket. Her shoes were black and, unlike my lace-up shoes, had narrow straps which went over her arches and buckled to the sides. But, it was her hair which I noticed in particular. It was the same colour as my own but, unlike my short, back, and sides, hers was long, loosely curled and cascaded over her shoulders to swirl around her face as she moved. And then she was gone as my mother relentlessly pulled me towards the waiting coaches. As my mother relentlessly pulled me towards the waiting coaches, the girl disappeared into the crowd.
>
> As we got closer to our coach, I noticed other families. A few of the women held their arms outstretched while holding their loved one's hands. As I looked up into the face of one of the women, I could see her staring into the eyes of her service-man husband. She stood transfixed by the immensity of the parting and then, in one smooth motion, he swept his kitbag onto his shoulder, followed us into the waiting coach, closed the door, lowered the window, and waved. He waved until his wife could no longer be seen.
>
> "Would you and your boy like this seat?" one of the soldiers asked my mother as he picked up his kitbag and swung it into the overhead rack.

My mother nodded. "I was worried about getting a seat. It takes awhile to get to Oxford."

"Are you visiting friends?" the soldier asked politely.

"I'm going to see my husband for the first time since he was shot. He's a paratrooper . . . perhaps I should say he was a paratrooper. He was shot in the leg on a drop in Italy." My mother then turned to me and asked, "Would you like your colouring book?"

I shook my head, pulled up my knee-high socks, and stuffed my green cap with its gold braid into the back pocket of my new-for-the-trip gray short trousers. I turned away from the soldier and stared out at the passing bombed-out buildings. I used my jacket's sleeve in an unsuccessful attempt to clean cigarette smoke from the inside of the window but gave up when I realized that most of the grime was on the outside. Then, my attention changed to the train. Ever since I had seen it enter the station, it seemed like a huge beast held captive by unknown people who forced it against its will to do their bidding. It puffed and wheezed in protest as its masters coaxed it into motion; its wheels had complained loudly as they alternatively slipped and grabbed the rails. But, as it gained speed, I sensed its anger at being forced to drag the coaches and the people within them subsiding. It became free. Now there was only effortless motion and the soothing clack of wheels on rails.

Then, my mother and I were walking through the park-like grounds of the hospital. As we walked through a grove of tall and stately trees, we discovered a pond. The path split and my mother and I separated as I chose the one that led to the water's edge. I felt at peace. It was the only place I had ever seen that didn't show the ravages of war. For a few minutes, wartorn England did not exist. As my mother walked on, I stopped and stared into the pond and looked at my reflection. I stared at long, loosely curled hair that cascaded over my shoulders and swirled around my face when I moved. And then, through misted eyes, I saw my shoes were black and had narrow straps which went over my arches and buckled to the sides. At the very core of my being, I ached to be a girl.

"Come on Michael," my mother said, as she waited where the two paths rejoined. "Stop daydreaming. Don't you want to see your father?"

The girl in the pond stared back at me for a moment longer, and then we parted. My mother and I walked across a lawn to the hospital. Once, it had been a stately home but, at the beginning of the war, it had been commandeered as a rehabilitation hospital for wounded servicemen. My father's bed was in a large room which opened onto a garden. His leg was wrapped in white bandages, held up at an angle by pulleys attached to the ceiling and his upper body was encased in plaster which, when I tapped on it, sounded like a drum. Strangely, I felt reassured; the solidity of the plaster confirmed that he was alive.

"Do you want to play cowboys and Indians?" my father asked, pulling me across the bed where I was sitting and onto his cast where I now found myself astride a horse. He bounced me up and down as best he could and I broke into bouts of laughter as I slapped the sides of my horse with my hands and dug my spurs into the bed. We played horsy until my father could play no longer.

"Do you want to play in the garden?" my father asked.

"Can I play by the pond?"

"You won't be safe there," my mother said. "You can play anywhere you like in the garden as long as you're not out of sight."

As I climbed one of the many trees in the garden, I could see my mother and father talking while she held his hand in both of hers. Then, it was time to go home. My mother hugged my father as best she could and kissed him. I climbed once more onto his cast and tapped it several times. Despite my protests, my father rubbed his stubbled chin across my face and deposited a wet kiss on my cheek. Then, we left.

We didn't walk through the grove of trees, but the girl in the pond was with me. I couldn't see her clearly in the train's smoke-stained window. But, she was with me.

References

Conrad, J. (2006). The nigger of the Narcissus. Retrieved July 20, 2020 from http://gutenberg.org/files/17731-h/17731-h.htm#link2H_PREF

Dillard, A. (1990). *Three by Annie Dillard: Pilgrim at Tinker Creek; An American childhood; The writing life.* Harper Perennial.

Fish, S. (1981). How to recognize a poem when you see one. In I. Konigsberg (Ed.), *American criticism in the poststructuralist age* (pp. 102–115). University of Michigan.

Grumet, M. (1988). *Bitter milk: Women and teaching.* University of Massachusetts Press.

Haug, F. (2000). *Memory-work as a method of social science research, a detailed rendering of memory work method.* http://www.friggahaug.inkrit.de/documents/memorywork-re-searchguidei7.pdf

Highsmith, P. (1952). *The price of salt.* Norton.

Johnson, S. (2004). *Mind wide open: Your brain and the neuroscience of everyday life.* Scribner.

Labonte, R., & Schimel, L. (2007). *First person queer: Who we are (so far).* Arsenal Pulp Press.

Lodge, D. (2002). *Consciousness and the novel.* Penguin.

Oliver, K. (2001). *Witnessing: beyond recognition.* University of Minnesota Press.

Rand, A, (2000). *The art of fiction.* Plume.

Robson, C. (2006). *Transformations: Collected Writings by the Quirk-e Collective.* Lulu.

Shields, C. (2002). *Unless.* Random House.

Sumara, D. (2002). *Why reading literature in school still matters: Imagination, interpretation, insight.* Lawrence Erlbaum.

Van Gulick, R. (2018, Spring). Consciousness. In *The Stanford Encyclopedia of Philosophy.* Retrieved July 20, 2020 from https://plato.stanford.edu/archives/spr2018/entries/consciousness

Varela, F. (1999). *Ethical know-how: Action, wisdom, and cognition.* Stanford University Press.

Winterson, J. (1995). *Art objects: Essays on ecstasy and effrontery.* Vintage Books.

Zunshine, L. (2006). *Why we read fiction: Theory of mind and the novel.* Ohio State University Press.

CHAPTER ELEVEN

Modes of Representation

There is a dialectic of withdrawal and extension, isolation and community,
assertion and submission to aesthetic practice that requires both the studio
where the artist harvests silence and the gallery where she serves the fruit
of her enquiry to others.

—Grumet (1988, p. 94)

IN THIS CHAPTER, I consider the particular representational demands made on collective community artists with a critical agenda: making art for social change. As Grumet (1988) reminds us in the chapter-opening epigraph, the studio in which the artist reflects and gathers insight is important, but so, too, is the gallery where the work is exhibited. Where art for social change is concerned, it is of particular importance how and where these representations are disseminated because of its aim to mobilize communities. In this chapter, I offer three examples of how the writing of various collectives was extended to broader audiences. Each demonstrates the ways in which the facilitator can best serve the work by paying attention to its intention and guiding it toward its most effective expression.

Art has always generated social change, even when this has not been its express purpose. One only has to consider the work of Joyce and Woolf, which both reflected and commented on early 20th-century investigations into the nature of identity as they captured the nuances and nature of internal dialogue and the processes of the human mind (Denzin, 2000; Lodge, 2002). It remains true, however, that socially engaged art has a particular responsibility to its audiences. When Freire (2000, p. 15) first used the term *critical pedagogy*, he did so in the belief that "education makes sense because women and men learn that through learning they can make and remake themselves." This project of "remaking" is not just concerned with the generation of individual understanding but with larger projects of social justice. The work that came out of Freire's emancipatory agenda, such as the political theater of Boal, Diamond, and others, offers prime examples of work that serves the needs of marginalized populations such as street youth, immigrants, and victims of domestic violence (Sandlin et al., 2010). Although they do offer important opportunities for individuals to express themselves and represent their lives, these projects serve a public, as well as a private, function as they offer ways to revitalize, advocate, and speak for the rights of communities and countercultures and make visible abstract social systems, such as class, family, religion, gender, and sexuality (Cvetkovich, 2003).

My own work as a community artist has tended to concentrate on the production of written memoir, and I begin all my projects with individual writing by participants, for three reasons. First, my education, training, and my own artistic practices have led me in that direction—it is what I do best. Second, I believe that it is an effective way to generate insight and understanding. Finally, writing is an accessible medium. Like soccer (as opposed to hockey or golf), it requires little in terms of technological or financial resources. However, I attempt to remain open to the most effective forms of representing the experiences that unfold through the working pedagogical structures I lead. This has led me to explore other ways and other places that participants can represent and disseminate the ideas and insights that emerge through critical life writing.

Patti Lather (1986, p. 67) has suggested that the validity of qualitative research can be measured partly by its ability to create social change and calls this capacity "catalytic validity." For the politically motivated arts facilitator, or organic intellectual, performance is not only a matter of showcasing the work but also a means to change hearts and minds. Where and how the work is shown matter in terms of its historical connotations and likely audience. A reading in a West Side LGBTQ bookstore is likely to attract allies, but a reading in a community center in Richmond (a more socially conservative part of Vancouver) may be less well attended but have a greater impact in terms of increasing visibility.

In the rest of this chapter, I illustrate some of the choices I have made in this regard.

1. Bill Morrow: *Homophobic Homo*

In 2012, the Quirk-e collective decided to produce an anthology of writing that represented queer life as it was experienced by members of the group through times of intense social change. Our title was *The Bridge Generation* (Robson & Blair, 2014), and our cover byline was "*A queer elders' chronicle from no rights to civil rights.*" Our plan was to organize our work together through four sections, each covering two decades of queer life (the 1940s and 1950s, the 1960s and 1970s, the 1980s and 1990s, and the 2000s and 2010s). The book was produced in collaboration with two departments from Simon Fraser University. Faculty from the departments of Gender Sexuality and Women's Studies and History helped us with research for the book, wrote introductions to each section, and gave financial and organizational assistance with its production. Members of the collective were highly en-gaged and enthusiastic about this project, which, as noted earlier, involved research at the Vancouver Public Library and was managed within the group by four editorial teams, one for each section.

One member of the group, Bill (now deceased), approached me early in the project to tell me that he felt the need to withdraw from Quirk-e. Bill was in his late 70s at this time, physically frail, and suffering some cognitive decline that made it difficult for him to write with clarity. He felt, therefore, that his usefulness to the project was limited and that he would "hold us back" in this important work (personal communication, May, 2012). This was not an easy decision on Bill's part—indeed, he saw himself as sacrificing his own sense of connection for the greater good of the collective, of which he was a loyal and committed member.

After some reflection, I challenged Bill's offer to withdraw as I appealed not to his own need for the group's support but to his responsibility to share his stories with a larger audience. I reminded him that as the oldest member of the group, his stories about rejection by his church community when he came out as a young man were vital to our project because he was the only one of us who grew up queer in Canada in the 1940s. Who else, I asked him, could write about what that was like? I suggested that, instead of leaving us, he might pair up with Judy Fletcher (see Chapter 2) to represent his ex-periences in a different way. Fortunately, we had been experimenting with a free online program, *Comic Life*, which allowed artists to import their own images and text into comic strips. Judy and Bill worked together to combine Bill's archival images with other images they researched together online. The following are the results of their collaboration.

Figure 11.1: *Homophobic Homo* by Bill Morrow and Judy Fletcher

Figure 11.2: *Homophobic Homo* by Bill Morrow and Judy Fletcher

Figure 11.3: *Homophobic Homo* by Bill Morrow and Judy Fletcher

Figure 11.4: *Homophobic Homo* by Bill Morrow and Judy Fletcher

This form of graphic representation builds on Bill's written memoir to tell his story succinctly and effectively. It returned his sense of agency and commitment to the group's social agenda. In addition, it generated a strong and enduring emotional bond between Judy (who has a tendency to isolate)

and Bill across the lines of gender. The inclusion of graphic work provided an interesting alternative to the dense text in the anthology and is au courant in its appeal to younger readers in a digital age.

2. Bridget Coll and Chris Morrissey: *A Poem in Two Voices*

When several members of Quirk-e developed dementia and memory loss, I responded by constructing a federally funded project that looked into the ways in which making art together about memory (both individual and collective) might strengthen the networks that support memory and shed light on the ways in which our memories serve in the construction of identity (Robson, 2014). Early in the project, Chris Morrissey and Bridget Coll, a long-standing lesbian couple, announced in one of our workshops that they would like to read us a poem they had composed in two blended voices (a form we had experimented with in previous years). Apparently, they had each talked with the seniors' worker at the community center where we met about what it was like to live together with Bridget's diagnosis of vascular dementia. They drew from the resulting transcripts to write the pastiche poem that follows. Although there has since been a wave of publicity about dementia, in these early days, it was almost a taboo topic, so the poem had great power and poignancy, especially for others in the group with similar diagnoses. Chris and Bridget's poem was a coming out of a different kind, and we were all somewhat lost for words as they finished reading their poem, which appears below.

"Memory in Two Voices," by Chris Morrissey and Bridget Coll

B.   It's not me, it's my disease.

C.   *It's not you, it's your disease*

C.   As I age, I wonder how my life will end. Bridget and I occasionally talk about which one of us will die first. Funny, we have never spoken about how we will die.

B.   *Chris wants me to go to the geriatric clinic for an assessment.*

C.   So often Bridget asks me, "Have you seen my keys? My bus pass? My library book? I just had that thing in my hand! Where did I put it?"

B. *I'm going to the library.*

C. I thought you were just there.

B. *Yes, I was. Someone just called to tell me I left my wallet.*

C. "Mild memory loss," the doctor says. Come back in a year."
Bridget had a lightness in her step. Not me. Even though I told
the person who did the interview and administered the test and
the doctor what I was noticing, I feel ignored. "Come back in a
year." A whole year.

B. *I cannot remember where Chris has gone. I'm sure she told me.
Where is she? Has something happened to her?*

C. *Are you OK? Where were you? Are you OK?* Every day, several times a day Bridget asks me.

I nag her. Turn out the light, close the door. Please put the milk
back in the fridge. Close the fridge door. She's getting worse. My
friend has told me that there is medication. *I* can't wait any longer.

I decide that we must get back to the clinic and I make an ap-
pointment to get another referral.

B. *Why is this happening to me? I feel scared.*

*Our second visit to the clinic. Another interview, the same tests.
A second visit with the doctor. "There has been a decline in your
memory. Looking directly at me she says, "You have dementia."*

C. That's it. No questions about how we are after receiving the
"diagnosis." No referrals. Nothing. We walk out together, side
by side. Silent.

B. *"Do people die of dementia?"*

C. Silence. I don't answer.

B. *Every day—I'm more dependent. I'm forbidden to use the
stove unless someone else is in the house.*

Why me?

B. & C. What does the future hold?

C. Sometimes I feel ashamed that at times I wonder about my future. About getting impatient.

B. *Will I get worse? Better? Stay the same? I'm scared. Will I be able to recognize people?*

C. We hold hands as we walk, especially as we cross the street. It's not like the old days when holding hands in the street was a public display of our relationship. No—now in those moments I experience her as a child. I hate feeling like that.

B. *Will I recognize Chris, my partner of 37 years?*

C. Where is my partner? I'm losing her. I miss her. Even now, she's not the same woman I have spent years with.

B. *I hate it when someone says to me "You forgot . . . whatever it is." It's a trigger; it reminds me of my frailty and I don't want to be reminded all the time. It's not helpful.*

   When people ask me how I am, I say, "Physically I'm fine. It's my memory that's not good."

C. I hate it when people say, "I forget things too." For, heaven's sake; it's just not the same.

B. *I can't say the word . . .*

C. dementia.

B. & C. We are learning to live from day to day—one day at a time.

B. *Some days I think I'm doing fine, especially when I remember to turn off a light or a faucet*

C. "For heaven's sake, why can't she remember . . . to turn off the water, to close the fridge door. Why is she so slow?"

   Remember it's not her, it's her disease.

B. *I'm grateful I don't get lost.*

C. Not yet.

B. *I can read the same book over and over and enjoy it.*

C. She's so positive. I wish I could always be the same. I continue
    to learn.

(Looking at each other)

B. & C. We constantly have to remind ourselves—

B. *It's not me*

C. It's your disease.

B. & C. It's OURS.

Immediately after the session, my assistant artist, Kelsey Blair, and I decided that we needed to film the two women reading the poem, as a matter
of urgency, before Bridget's cognition deteriorated further. The next day, I
spent my entire Social Sciences and Humanities Research Council of Canada
(SSHRCC) postdoctoral research budget ($4,000 CA) on a high-quality video
camera, memory card, and microphone, and we set up a recording session
a few days later. In the raw footage that results, Bridget's voice is indistinct,
and Chris has to remind her partner several times where she is on the page.
Although we had archived this extraordinary work, we believed it needed
a wider audience but acknowledged a dilemma. Although the poem would
appear in print in our upcoming anthology, we both felt it worked better as
a live performance. Bridget was tiny and frail at this point, and seeing her
struggle to articulate is an important part of receiving the words she speaks.
We also knew that it would reach a larger audience as a movie because film
is a highly portable medium. However, Bridget's lack of clarity as a reader
rendered the video footage difficult to understand, and her declining cognition
made the possibility of future live performances questionable.

We also had an ethical issue. We felt that the work exposed Bridget's
frailty in a way that made us uncomfortable. Members of the group were
used to sharing their vulnerabilities in public, but in this case, it felt too
much. Kelsey and I were protective of Bridget's dignity. Accordingly, we
asked Chris and Bridget how they would feel about letting others read the
work, but Bridget was particularly reluctant. She agreed that the poem was

emotionally exposing but was convinced that the audience needed to hear the work in her voice. "It will have more impact," she said to us, "if I read it myself." Like Bill, she was committed to our mission for social change.

In the end, we thought outside the box. I contacted two improvisational dancers I knew from Simon Fraser University (Celeste Snowber and Kathryn Rickets), and they agreed to collaborate (without payment) on a film project. We rented studio space and played the soundtrack from our video of Bridget and Chris reading the poem in the background as the dancers interpreted it through spontaneous improvisation (all this happened within 3 weeks of the initial reading to the group). Kelsey spliced together clips of Chris and Bridget's reading with clips of the two dancers improvising on it. The soundtrack represents the text of the entire poem as read by its authors, but Kelsey provided visual captions throughout so that the viewer could hear and see the poem in its entirety. The film screened at The Vancouver Parks' Board Arts and Health Showcase, the Vancouver Public Library, and as part of AGEWELL, presented by Arts for Social Change. For a while, Chris and Bridget became "poster children" for dementia. They were interviewed on public radio and helped raise awareness of the illness in the Lower Mainland of Canada.

Bridget died in 2016, and the video was shown at her funeral. As a side note, at least four celebrations of life for Quirk-e members have included artwork composed by the deceased artist or by others in the collective. This speaks to the importance of art as it contributes to the creation of alternative rituals and celebrations for those who have lived outside normative structures.

3. Syd Wolfe: *The Queer Agenda*

In 2014, Quirk-e partnered with Youth for A Change (YfAC), a group of young lesbian, gay, bisexual, trans*, and queer youth (ages 13–22) from Surrey who want to make a difference by educating the public about queer concerns and issues and advocating for queer rights. We believed that the partnership represented what Grumet would describe as an *extension* of Quirk-e's work, as it addressed a significant cultural gap. In the normal course of events, Syd and the members of Quirk-e would not be likely to even meet, given the generational divide between young and older queers.

Queer youth are less likely than other youth to have contact with their parents and grandparents, and queer seniors are less likely than other seniors to be supported by their children or grandchildren, if they even have them (LGBT Movement Advance Project & SAGE, 2010). Queer youth are also less likely than their heterosexual age peers to meet and interact with older, nonkin individuals who identify as queer. Although much of what we learn about healthy relationships is communicated through the wisdom, examples, and stories of our elders, queer youth are often denied access to these, both in terms of formal and informal education (Boulay et al., 2014; Cherry-Reid, 2015). Narratives of pedophilia have not helped as they have made us all concerned about the perception, if not the reality, of exploitation.

The pedagogical theories and feminist principles fundamental to Quirk-e were used to inform a collaborative project between the two groups: a full-length theater performance called *Intergen(d)erational*. The show was performed in Vancouver and Surrey in the spring of 2015 and then remounted by invitation at New Westminster Pride in 2015. It included a piece called *The Queer Agenda* written and performed by YfAC member Sydney (Syd) Oremek, a queer punk teen who was homeless for 3 years and was a Grade 9 dropout because of homophobic bullying. *The Queer Agenda* (reprinted with permission) speaks back to religious fundamentalism and was the closing number of the full-length performance. The following is the entire text:

The Queer Agenda, by Sydney Oremek

I am here to corrupt your kids, destroy your marriage, and end all peace and order as you know it. Hello, my name is the queer agenda. I am the thing that middle-aged white man fears. I am the whisper in the night—equality! Queer! I am the rock of liberation thrown into the glass wall of corruption and mistreatment. For a long time now, I have been gathering Intel on what you, the ordinary people, hold dear to heart. You cherish your ignorance. If you pretend it is not there, then it simply has no other choice than to disappear, correct? WRONG! That is where I, the queer agenda, shall invade and plant the bomb that will explode your mind. My warriors call it 'being open minded. Queer! *maniacal laugh* Yes! We shall invade your mind and with us bring all the rainbows and sparkles that we can dare carry, and we shall march to the top of your brain and plant our rainbow flags deep in your mind, and claim this land, IN THE NAME OF ALL THINGS EQUAL AND FREE!

Come

(Everyone steps forward)

My army of homosexuals will then stand back and watch as the ordinary suburban household crumbles and with it everything good and sane.

(Everyone walks up behind them).

It will begin with the men trading in their beers at the local pub for a pomegranate martini at the clubs; their dirty old blue jeans and lumberjack shirt to be exchanged for bright blue denim cut-offs and a vee-necked shirt. The women will begin cutting off all their hair, stop shaving, and wear pants. And as the men slowly stop doing their hard 'dirty' work and instead apply for jobs as secretaries, the women will bear-to-arms a hammer and tool belt with which they will construct the rainbow houses of the future. Gay pride parades will happen on all streets everyday, as people decorate themselves with "Born this way" tee-shirts and place rainbow pride flags in front of every house.

All marriages would fail, causing mass divorce in the world. Babies would stop being born because the men would refuse to touch the women and the women would refuse to even be in the same room as a man. There would be riots because of the escalating number of new-found-gays who would want to get married and the government would finally have to start listening to the demands of their country. Everything heterosexual would cease to exist and the world would crumble into a rainbow black hole of total gay-dom.

And that would be it. The extinction of the heterosexual race. Ladies and gentlemen, women and men, badass bitches, and sissy boys:

Chorus: I am the queer agenda, and you have just heard my roar.

In terms of its content, *The Queer Agenda* takes a homophobic meme— the ideas that queers want to take over and pervert the world—and stands it on its head in an act of ironic queer reclaiming. Queer youth and elders are often seen purely in terms of being frail and at risk (of such things as depression, suicide, isolation, and homelessness). Syd's work positioned them as powerful (even dangerous) producers of social goods and as change makers. Again, however, I want to draw attention to the ways in which it worked better as performed art, rather than text on a page in our anthology, although it was also published that way (Robson et al., 2017).

It is one thing to read this amusing piece and quite another to see it performed on a stage packed with queer youth and elders adorned with gay regalia and flags, especially at the moment where Syd, its young narrator, issues the invitation to her Rainbow Army to step forward into battle and the entire cast marches forward in a deeply symbolic gesture. We performed the piece several times, and the contexts of these performances were important: Kwantlen Polytechnic University in Surrey (a city where queer voices have not always been welcomed), Britannia Community Centre (a traditional site of queer visibility and activism), and New Westminster Gay Pride (a queer context for sure but one that has typically failed to include the voices of the old and the young). Although the piece "read" differently in each location, audience members in each venue commented on how unusual and inspirational it was to see young and older lesbian, gay, bisexual, and transgender people come together in this performance. At one performance, a representative from a local union offered, on the spot, significant financial support for our future work. For grassroots projects such as ours, the need to secure funding is an important reality.

The Queer Agenda was useful in other ways. Activist art in alternative, nonpedagogical spaces can be viewed as particularly important to our youth and elder participants, many of whom, youth and elders alike, were bullied or otherwise marginalized in their previous learning situations or spent periods out of school. For the youth, particularly, it demonstrated the impact of the written word and the possibility and the power of community art making. Both YfAC and Quirk-e are still making and showing their art at the time of writing.

Finally, this project offered a third fictive space in which youth and elders talked about central issues. At one point, some members of Quirk-e were reluctant to take the stage because they disliked the notion of wishing for the "extinction of the heterosexual race." The debate led us into heated discussion of several key issues and questions: Why do youth look the way they do? How can humor/satire be mobilized positively? Where is the line between censorship and potentially hateful speech? Ultimately, they came to understand the piece as an ironic reflection on fundamentalism and an expression of the kind of rage that many "young" movements need to express. If the piece has been offered purely as disembodied text, I doubt that these important conversations would have occurred.

I have argued that an important part of art making is that the artist pays close attention to the intention of the work that is emerging. In this chapter, I have suggested that the ways in which facilitators and educators guide and structure the flow of creativity in the collaborations they manage depend on the same kind of sensitivity to emergent work. Rather than imposing their own agendas, they need to pay attention to the art and allow it to inform the agenda of the collective, staying light on their feet so that they can adapt their pedagogical plans. Eisner (1996, 2002) has suggested, and I agree, that teachers are themselves artists who are flexibly purposeful, "capitalizing on the emergent features appearing within a field of relationships" and not "rigidly attached to predefined aims when the possibility of better ones emerge" (Eisner, 2002, para 27). They see that form and content are often inextricable—"one of the lessons," Eisner (2002, para 30) suggests, "that the arts teach most profoundly." They strike a fine balance between pedagogical approaches that are laissez-faire and those that are overly directive. These choices are conducted within the field of relationships, and they must remain open and sensitive to these. Oliver (2001) would call this a form of response-ability.

References

Boulay, N., Yeung, B., Leung, C., & Burns, P. (2014). LGBTQ Role models and curricular controversy in Canada: A student symposium. *Paideusis, 22*(1), 19–27.

Cherry-Reid. K. (2015). *Singing queer: archiving and constructing a lineage through song* [Unpublished dissertation]. University of British Columbia.

Cvetkovich, A. (2003). *An archive of feelings: Trauma, sexuality, and lesbian public cultures.* Duke University Press.

Denzin, N. K. (2000). The art and politics of interpretation. In N. K. Denzin & Y. S. Lincoln (Eds.), *Handbook of qualitative research* (pp. 500–515). Sage Publications.

Eisner, E. W. (1996). Is "the art of teaching" a metaphor? In M. Kompf, W. R. Bond, D. Dworet, & R. T. Boak (Eds.), *Changing research and practice: Teachers' professionalism identities and knowledge* (pp. 9–20). Falmer Press.

Eisner, E. W. (2002). What can education learn from the arts about the practices of education? In *Encyclopedia of informal education.* Retrieved July 20, 2020 from http://www.infed.org/biblio/eisner_arts_and_the_practice_of_education.htm

Freire, P. (2000). *Pedagogy of the oppressed*. Continuum.

Grumet, M. (1988). *Bitter milk: Women and teaching*. University of Massachusetts Press.

Lather, P. (1986). Issues of validity in openly ideological research: Between a rock and a soft place. *Interchange of Educational Policy, 17*(4), 63–84. doi:10.1007/BF01807017

LGBT Movement Advance Project & SAGE. (2010, March). *Improving the lives of LGBT older adults*. https://www.lgbtmap.org/improving-the-lives-of-lgbt-older-adults

Lodge, D. (2002). *Consciousness and the novel*. Penguin.

Oliver, K. (2001). *Witnessing: Beyond recognition*. University of Minnesota Press.

Robson, C. (2014). The memory project. Unpublished raw data.

Robson, C., & Blair, K. (Eds.) (2014). *The bridge generation*. Lulu.

Robson, C., Blair, K., & Marchbank, J. (Eds.) (2017). *Basically queer: An intergenerational introduction to LGBTQA2S+ lives*. Peter Lang.

Sandlin, J. A., Schultz, B. D., & Burdick, J. (2010). *Handbook of public pedagogy: Education and learning beyond schooling*. Routledge.

CHAPTER TWELVE

The Ethics of Working Through

There is something in critique which is akin to virtue.
—Foucault (1990/1997, p. 25)

IN THIS CHAPTER, I return to Oliver's (2001) suggestion that the essential nature and dynamic of human subjectivity are relational, rather than oppositional, as I consider some of the ethical issues involved in collaborative art making for social change. When we frame collective art making as a means of working through and repairing both the overt and insidious traumas of oppression, injustice, and marginalization and the construction of sustainable relationships with others, then there are important implications for our educational and research projects. When subjectivity is seen as existing within an energetic relational field, we are obligated to treat others in ways that open up the possibility of address and response (Oliver, 2001, p. 15). Rather than just *recognizing* the experiences of others (which can still be a form of "othering"), we *witness* those experiences, as we *work through* hostilities and find compassion.

In his analysis of *parrhesia*, or "fearless speech," Foucault (1988) traces the origins of the term back through its genealogy from its origins in early resistance to the totalizing dogma of the church. Although its meanings have shifted in the historical contexts in which they were used and constructed, he offers the following overall definition:

> *Parrhesia* is a kind of verbal activity where the speaker has a specific relation to truth through frankness, a certain relationship to his own life through danger, a certain type of relation to himself or other people

through criticism (self-criticism or criticism of other people), and a specific relation to moral law through freedom and duty. (Foucault, 1988, p. 19)

In the quotation that opens this chapter, Foucault (1990/1997) suggests a connection between critique and virtue, as the subjugated have a moral duty to speak truth to power, even when there is a risk involved in challenging normative discourses. Those who engage in democratic parrhesia to criticize dominant cultures do so because they recognize that truth telling is a duty because it not only helps individuals to desubjugate themselves and achieve a level of autonomy but also improves and helps other people.

Oliver (2001) takes this argument a step further, as she challenges the dichotomy between subject and other or subject and object. Oliver (2001, p. 11) believes that "subjectivity is not the result of exclusion" and that we have created "an impossible problem for ourselves by presuming to be separated in the first place" (p. 12). The problem of othering is "itself a result of the pathology of oppression" (Oliver, 2001, p. 3), which leads to dehumanization. Like Foucault, Oliver suggests that taking up a position as speaking subjects can repair damaged subjectivity, but she takes a crucial next step by defining subjectivity as inherently relational and contextual. Identity is navigated in relationships with others rather than in attempts to be separate from them.

My argument throughout this book has been that the processes of remembering, recognizing, and representing are complex, embodied, and interrelated. Vision is a process of constant revisions, and what and how we see is influenced not only by what we have already seen and experienced but also by the cultural web of relationships that have formed and continue to form and shape us. "The intellect," Oliver (2001, p. 2) argues, is not separate from "perception, sensation, passion, or embodiment in general," and we are not separate from each other. To see human relationships as an antagonistic struggle for recognition leads any search for democratic, peaceful, or ethical relationships into a reductionist dead end. Rather, we could more productively view human relationships as existing in a field of social and affective energy, as many Indigenous people have for centuries (Archibald, 2008).

When art making for social change is seen through this theoretical lens, there are implications for our practices. First, there is the business of difference and how it can not only be acknowledged but also embraced and enjoyed. Although both young and old queer communities are often essentialized in popular public discourses, key differences exist in identifications, in terms of gender, sexual orientation (including asexuality and bisexuality), education, age, and political beliefs. Both Youth for A Change and Quirk-e are consciously inclusive of all genders and orientations and open to those with diagnoses of physical, emotional, and mental ill health and varied educational backgrounds and artistic "abilities." In each group, this has led to rich new understandings of differences in terms of ability, political perspectives, and the various normalizing discourses we have internalized about gender, age, and sexuality. These engagements in acts of response and address are of particular importance in queer culture, which has tended to maintain silos in terms of both recreational and intellectual and political activities.

However, working through differences has also been difficult on occasion, as it has involved the navigation of conflicts, sideways hostilities, the consequences of trauma, illness, and physical and mental frailty. To "see others with loving eyes that invite [a] loving response . . . demands constant vigilance towards responsibility in relationships" (Oliver, 2001, p. 19). I have outlined some of the strategies my groups have developed to construct and maintain these relationships (see Chapter 5). Here I wish to emphasize that these are strategies that do not just "help" the work but also lie at its very heart.

When the teacher/researcher cannot be regarded as separate from student/participant but as part of the collective, this also has implications for practice. In Chapter 5, I theorized the role (following Haug and Gramsci) as that of the organic or embedded intellectual: someone who shares the mission and social agenda of the collective but brings their particular skills and expertise (often the consequence of privilege) to the group's work. This position can be difficult to negotiate as tensions emerge.

For instance, I am usually more concerned than my participants about the need to package and promote the work in ways that will appeal to funders, and I have more experience than most, although not all, of my participants of the ways in which educational, activist, and health care funders operate and prioritize and, thus, how to leverage resources. This situation has made me more constrained and pragmatic in my planning but, at the same time (arguably), is more likely to encourage experimentation, as I have constantly invited the group to expand its repertoire and explore new forms of expression likely to interest funders, including the construction of the memory box collection, a human library, and the inclusion of graphic work in our anthologies. As far as possible, I have been transparent about the rationale for each project and the ways in which it also connects with our mission, and I have involved members of the group in writing many of the grants we have applied for through the formation of a grant-writing committee. It must be acknowledged, however, that despite my attempts to explain the realities of funding, I have encountered resistance from members of the group from time to time, as they have balked at the demands that I have made on them and seen some of our projects (including our intergenerational collaborations) as an unwelcome distraction from their individual work.

When teacher-researchers see themselves this way, the question of objectivity becomes at once more and less meaningful. In her article "Do I Like Them too Much?" Valerie Yow (1997) has questioned the possibility of objectivity in recording lived oral history, but for organic intellectuals, working alongside and with others with a shared agenda, the question goes beyond that as it becomes one of seeking response-ability rather than objectivity. This does not mean that they can sidestep the issue of objectivity entirely. When they have an investment in the group's mission, it is even more important to pay close attention to their individual biases and blind spots, to encourage and listen to dissenting or quiet voices, to member-check publications, and to temperature-test the mood. It can be a difficult balance to allow for individual differences while finding and nurturing consensus and, at the same time, acknowledge one's own investment in the outcome of the work. I believe that I have invited questions, comments, and criticisms from my participants more than is usual for most facilitators. I also believe that this has led to more authentic and trusting relationships. Although it is difficult to describe or define the close understanding and sensitivity that the collective arts facilitator develops with those she works with and the trust that is developed among all participants, it is a vital ingredient for successful projects.

Traditional approaches to maintaining ethical relationships with participants do not work well in participatory action research, of which arts activism for social change can be seen as a subset. As Blake (2007, p. 414) has pointed out, most institutional ethics review procedures position the researched as "needful of protection because they lack discrimination." She adds that it would be unusual to include consultations around ethical procedures with representatives from the community being researched or even the nonacademic public. In their attempts to "protect" participants from breaches of confidentiality, ethics review committees can make it extremely difficult for researchers to give voice to underrepresented populations by giving them ownership of their artistic productions. All of the artists whose work appears in this book have requested that their actual names be used, and this is a typical response but one that has proved almost inconceivable for those granting institutional ethical approval. This can be particularly problematic when using images of those perceived as "at risk," such as queer youth and elders. This assumption that harm and exploitation may result from research projects comes from a place of othering (of researcher and researched) that is essentially antagonistic and does not acknowledge the embedded nature of the researcher (dismissed as "going native"), the engagement of the researched, and the complex relations forged outside the institution in the project. It denies visibility to those who have already been rendered invisible.

When we frame art activism as a fractal process of social engagement, it spills beyond the walls of the classroom or workshop as the work extends into the wider community. This means that it is always conducted with a view to finding and moving audiences and creating new publics and counterpublics (Warner, 2002). It also means that it is important to locate the work in strong community partnerships because this offers opportunities for dissemination, resources, publicity, and new ways of thinking and theorizing. Quirk-e was a simple, unknown writing group until it became part of the City of Vancouver's Arts & Health program. This web of connections included a vibrant community of practice for socially engaged artists, a curated annual show, and funding that allowed me to offer workshops free to all participants in an accessible public space.

One of our projects, *Raising Awareness and Addressing Elder Abuse in the LGBT Community: An Intergenerational Project* (Robson et al., 2018), offers a useful illustration of some of these points. The project engaged queer youth and elders in the design and production of digital videos and posters that raised awareness of elder abuse in the queer population (see Figures 12.1–12.3 for examples of the posters). Here is a link to all of the materials, including the three videos: https://www.sfu.ca/lgbteol/lgbt-elder-abuse-2.html.

Figure 12.1: Financial Abuse Poster, Front

Figure 12.2: Emotional Abuse Poster, Front

Although the intergenerational elder abuse project was modestly fund-ed ($55,000 CA, provided by a grant from the BC Council to Reduce Elder Abuse (CREA), it has had a significant impact. The materials produced (the

LGBTQ Elder Abuse: What do you know?

What is Elder Abuse?

Elder abuse occurs when people in positions of trust harm elders, either through their actions or their failure to act.

What is Financial Abuse?

Action or lack of action with respect to material possessions, funds, assets, property or legal documents, that is unauthorized or coerced, or a misuse of legal authority.*

Who Commits Elder Abuse?

- Private households (family, lovers, friends, children, neighbours, caregivers).
- Institutions such as hospitals, care homes, and assisted living (staff, visitors, other residents).

Why are Older LGBTQ People More Vulnerable to Abuse?

- Stigma and prejudice makes them an "invisible population"
- They are twice as likely to be single, aging alone
- They are less likely to have children or find them supportive
- They are more likely to have experienced trauma; and to have abused drugs and alcohol.

Why are LGBTQ People Less Likely to Report Abuse?

- They may not wish to give others even more cause to criticize them.
- They may not be out.

Where to find help or further information

If you are in immediate danger, call 9-1-1.

Seniors Abuse & Information Line at the BC Centre for Elder Advocacy & Support: 604.437.1940 or 1.866.437.1940 (toll free)

Fraser Health: 1-877-733-2808 or visit www.fraserhealth.ca/your_care/adult_abuse_and_neglect/

Interior Health: For direct community numbers visit www.interiorhealth.ca/reportabuse

Island Health: South Island: 1-888-533-2273. Central Island 1-877-734-4101. North Island 1-866-928-4988

Northern Health: Prince George Adult Protection Line 250-565-7414

Vancouver Coastal Health: ReAct Adult Protection Program 1-877-732-2899

* Abuse Definitions: National Initiative for Care of the Elderly 2013

Figure 12.3: Information (reverse of all posters)

first in Canada on this much-neglected topic) are now used in trainings by organizations in British Columbia (BC) and beyond, we have published our conclusions (Gutman et al., 2020; Robson et al., 2018) and presented at a number of conferences in Canada and the United Kingdom, as well as several community events.

As I analyze the project's success, I offer the following conclusions: First, the project was located centrally in the community it investigates, as it was conducted and disseminated through a number of partnerships and alliances with organizations that included the BC Council to Reduce Elder Abuse (our funders), QMUNITY (a nonprofit LGBTQ/2S organization), the Department of Gerontology at Simon Fraser University, Britannia Community Centre, the Arts & Health Project, and the five health regions of BC (Fraser Health, Interior Health, Northern Health, Vancouver Coastal Health, and Island Health). One of the three videos was filmed at Haro Park, a seniors' residential center.

Second, the project positioned youth and elders as resilient change makers instead of frail victims in need of help. One of the first decisions we made when planning the project was to dedicate funds in our budget to cover travel and accommodation for youth and elder participants who traveled across BC (to all five health regions) to speak at town-hall meetings to representatives from local health and community organizations. We found that very little thought had been given by many of these organizations to LGBTQ elder abuse, and there was a strong interest in our materials, which were made freely available at these events. We screened the videos, and youth and elders took the lead in the lively question-and-answer sessions that followed. By this time, they had close knowledge of the topic and thus became experts on a topic in the expert field of health care (one that has typically been experienced as adversarial by many LGBTQ people).

Youth and elders developed important skills, not only in terms of writing scripts, filming, acting, editing, and directing but also in public speaking. For the youth, particularly, this was an important education. We needed their film and artwork to be as professional as possible (while honoring their artistic ownership) and thus constantly challenged them to improve it. This was frustrating for them at times, but they learned some tough lessons about how to accept blunt feedback, negotiate, and take things less personally. For their part, some of the adults involved in the project learned to let go of their institutional power and to respect the reluctance of the youth to just do as they were told.

Rather than learning important skills in isolation and for the sake of it (such as writing scripts, filming, editing, speaking in public, and fielding questions), they learned them on the ground and in order to effect real and permanent social change. Their artistic decisions mattered because they sent important signals about representation. They needed to decide, for instance, who to feature in the posters. Lesbians, who are traditionally underrepresented? Transsexuals, for the same reason? Should the captions focus entirely on sexual/gender identifications or indicate that those pictured inhabit intersectional identifications? And what about race and ethnicity? Interestingly, it proved impossible to recruit any people from visible minorities to pose for the posters, despite our robust connections with communities of racialized others. In this way, we learned how multiple layers of stigma operate in racialized communities.

Finally, we learned that is was impossible to frame this project as research, for the reasons given earlier. The only "youth" who were able to act or narrate in the videos or attend the town halls were those who were legally adults. Even with these provisos, we would never have steered this project through an academic ethics review and thus framed it, instead, as a community project. This kind of work explodes the boundaries of traditional ethics protocols and suggests a pressing need for the construction of new ethical frameworks that acknowledge that it is relational, rather than antagonistic, and that participants are co-researchers rather than "subjects." Consent might be negotiated in ways that allow participants to be consulted ahead of time and given the opportunity to claim ownership of their work as well as ask for anonymity. Rather than conducting short-term kamikaze excursions into communities to collect "data," researchers might be encouraged to show how their work will mobilize knowledge, build agency and skills, forge new connections and partnerships, and mobilize communities. Such an approach would also require a reframing of the notion of research validity, as Lather (1986) has argued. It is work that calls into question our methodologies as we rethink such notions as triangulation and member checking. It also demands that we consider the needs of participants after our research has been concluded. What can we do to ensure that catalytic change is sustainable for the groups we have worked with? How can their voices and insights be heard in the dissemination of results, particularly in the elitist context of academic literature and expensive conferences?

To adopt Oliver's (2001) notion of "working through" helps us to find answers to these questions. The purpose of our teaching and our research becomes a matter of lending voice and agency to our participants around questions and issues that directly concern them. It involves response-ability and address-ability for everyone involved in the project. Crucially, it achieves catalytic validity by leaving those involved better off than they were at the start of the project as it generates sustainable change in their community.

References

Archibald, J-A./Q'um Q'um Xiiem (2008). *Indigenous storywork: Educating the heart, mind, body, and spirit*. UBC Press.

Blake, M. (2007). Formality and friendship: Research ethics review and participatory action research. *ACME: An international E-Journal for Critical Geographies, 6*(3), 411–421. https://acme-journal.org/index.php/acme/article/view/789

Foucault, M. (1988). Technologies of the self. In M. Luther, H. Gutman, & P. Hutton (Eds.), *Technologies of the self: A seminar with Michel Foucault* (pp. 16–49). University of Massachusetts Press.

Foucault, M. (1997). What is critique? (L. Hochroth, Trans.). In S. Lotringer & L. Hochroth (Eds.), *The politics of truth*. Semiotext(e). (Original work published 1990)

Gutman, G., Robson, C., & Marchbank, J. (2020). Elder abuse in the LGBT community. In A. Phelan (Ed.) *Advances in elder abuse: International perspectives on aging* (pp. 149–164). Springer.

Lather, P. (1986). Issues of validity in openly ideological research: Between a rock and a soft place. *Interchange, 17*, 63–84. doi:10.1007/BF01807017

Oliver, K. (2001). *Witnessing: beyond recognition.* University of Minnesota Press.

Robson, C., Gutman, G., Marchbank, J., & Blair, K. (2018). Raising awareness and addressing elder abuse in the LGBT community: An intergenerational project. *Language and Literacy, 20*(3), 46–66.

Warner, M. (2002). Publics and counterpublics. *Quarterly Journal of Speech, 88*(4), 413–425.

Yow, V. (1997). "Do I like them too much?" Effects of the oral history interview on the interviewer and vice-versa. *Oral History Review, 24*(1), 55–79.

CLOSING

The shaved privet is flat and bristly like Dad's face on Sundays. Most of the leaves are snipped across but I want a whole one, so my hand sneaks into the inside place where the shears never go. I find a round, undamaged leaf and pluck it. It is bad to pick things in the garden and to squash them. I have something private—a secret of my very own. I roll it between my fingers and its softness comforts me.

—Robson (2006, p. 59)

A s HUMAN BEINGS, WE inhabit spaces that are encultured, pruned, and regulated. At the same time, we are curious—we have evolved through constantly testing the limits and boundaries laid down by our cultural scripts and our available language. However, those of us whose lives do not fit the script and thus write under erasure must work harder to find a coherent through line. I have argued that one way to do this work is to reach beyond the regulated spaces we inhabit into interior psychic spaces that seem taboo and frightening but are filled with fertile surprises—juice and eggs. In many ways, the trick is a kind of letting go of sense and reason as the hand seems to move on its own. We cannot edit before we have composed. What we think we know will change. This kind of reaching is a form of hope in that it is impossible to hope if one does not believe that change will occur and unnecessary to hope if one is content with things the way they are.

Critical arts practices for social and individual change do not just *represent* what we believe to be true; they also help us to move beyond the single story and into more complex understandings. We revise what we write, and in the process, we are ourselves revised. As social beings, we work best with others, particularly when it comes to emotional work, but there are conditions in which this work best thrives, and where collective arts projects are concerned, they are quite particular because the work can be fragile and difficult. In this book, I have not offered a blueprint for the work of collective art making but, rather, a rationale and some methods that grow from it. It is my hope that these will prove helpful for other writers, artists, teachers, and students who believe, as do I, that making art can change both ourselves and our world.

I end by returning to "Privet" (Robson, 1996).

Here, as a reminder, is the analysis I offered in Chapter 1: "I did not speak out or fight against the domestic structures that conscribed me. Instead, I hurt and destroyed something tiny, fragile, and innocent. Its death throes repulsed me and filled me with horror at my own misdirected anger" (p. 13). I now see that this is both true and not true. In writing this book, I have thought my way past the single story and into a more complete understanding. I have practiced what I have been preaching.

I was that sad child in the front garden waving good-bye to my brother, captive to my mother's project: to bind my hands, to make me suitably female, suitably acquiescent. At the same time, I was an investigator, an outlier, and an iconoclast. I had the desire to reach inside, where the shears do not go, and wild things exist in their wholeness. I acknowledged the need to seize on to something that was mine, even if I had been told that it was wrong. I did not acquiesce. I was capable of transgression and anger. Even as an obedient child, I practiced disobedience. Even though I was constrained, I moved beyond the pale. I was waiting for the right circumstances, the right environment, the right education, but I was there all along.

I did not recognize these things at the time the incident happened. I did not recognize them when I first wrote "Privet" years later. I did not recognize them when I began writing this book. Now I am at the end, I can see things better.

Across the years, I give myself a wave.

Reference

Robson, C. (1996). Privet. In R. Elwin (Ed.), *Countering the myths* (pp. 57–61). Women's Press.

ABOUT THE AUTHOR

CLAIRE ROBSON is a writer, researcher, and arts activist. Her awards include Xtra West Writer of the Year, the Joseph Katz Memorial Scholarship (for her contributions to social justice), and the Lynch History Prize (for her contributions to better understanding of gender and sexual minorities). Claire is an adjunct faculty member at Simon Fraser University, in the Department of Gender, Sexuality, and Women's Studies. She has worked as an arts facilitator in academic and community contexts that include libraries, living rooms, community centers, and political organizations.

INDEX